From the wilds of the Minnesota woods, Gary Paulsen writes of a unique way of life, which he and his family have shared for the past several years. As a born-again Nature Boy, he recalls his "past life" fighting the Establishment, and his decision to take to the woods.

With humor and conviction, Paulsen tells why he did it—and how anyone else can adapt to "living lightly."

For those longing for greater meaning and enrichment to their existence, here is an alternative to the madness of the monetary system—how not to just make it, but actually improve by taking one step backward and coming out about four steps ahead. It's all possible in

BEAT THE SYSTEM:
A SURVIVAL GUIDE

ATTENTION: SCHOOLS AND CORPORATIONS

PINNACLE Books are available at quantity discounts with bulk purchases for educational, business or special promotional use. For further details, please write to: SPECIAL SALES MANAGER, Pinnacle Books, Inc., 1430 Broadway, New York, NY 10018.

WRITE FOR OUR FREE CATALOG

If there is a Pinnacle Book you want—and you cannot find it locally—it is available from us simply by sending the title and price plus 75¢ to cover mailing and handling costs to:

> Pinnacle Books, Inc.
> Reader Service Department
> 1430 Broadway
> New York, NY 10018

Please allow 6 weeks for delivery.

_____Check here if you want to receive our catalog regularly.

BEAT THE SYSTEM:

A SURVIVAL GUIDE

Gary Paulsen

PINNACLE BOOKS NEW YORK

BEAT THE SYSTEM: A SURVIVAL GUIDE

Copyright © 1982 by Gary Paulsen

All rights reserved, including the right to reproduce this book or portions thereof in any form.

An original Pinnacle Books edition, published for the first time anywhere.

First printing, December 1982

ISBN: 0-523-41317-3

Printed in the United States of America

PINNACLE BOOKS, INC.
1430 Broadway
New York, New York 10018

CONTENTS

Introduction 1
1 Changing Your Thinking 11
2 Realigning Your Value Base 23
3 Getting *Some* Money 39
4 Living Space 59
5 Getting Food 91
6 Building Knowledge and Getting By 113
7 Cars 129
8 Health—The Body—Clothing—The Mind—
   Hunting Deals 143
9 Living the Old Ways 159
10 Learning the Old Ways 171
11 Rib-sticking Recipes 197
12 How to Live on Just Absolutely Almost
   Nothing 223

INTRODUCTION

It comes to people in many different ways, couched in many different forms of language:

We're going to have to cut back.
We're going to have to tighten up.
We're going to have to restructure.
We're going to have to lose deadwood.
We're going to have to pare down.
Pick up your check.
Don't let the door hit you in the rear on the way out.

Some subtle, some blunt; the knowledge that you're about to join the ranks of the cut-back, tightened-up, pared-down, restructured poor has only one primary point—when they say *we*, they really mean *you*. And when you find that you're among those of us in the growing class of poor (or any other of the dozens of terms that can be used—lower class, under-incomed, etc.), the impact is almost always initially numbing.

This realization came for us in the flats east

and south of Denver, Colorado. We were fortunate in that it was softened by the complete and positive added knowledge that the system classing us as poor was no longer a system we wished to be involved with—not that we hadn't tried our best to make it work for us.

We had done it all. House in town (with chunky mortgage); two cars (to show our idiocy, they were both Pintos); a yacht (26-foot sloop in Ventura, California), expensive clothes; and (cream) eighty acres of scenic land for building our dream home, overlooking the Bijou Basin in Colorado.

All monthly payments that had to be met. God, how we scrambled when the payments came due, clawing and ripping to get enough money for each payment—tearing into each other when we (usually) fell short.

Perhaps twice in seven years we actually made all the payments on time. No more than that. More often it was a juggle—throw the envelopes in the air and pay the ones that landed on edge was the basic system we employed. And yet somehow we did it; we squeaked and bit and pulled and borrowed and begged and almost always somehow . . . just . . . barely . . . got . . . by.

And then the oil companies started.

Or maybe it was the utilities.

Then again it might have been the banks and their insane interests rates. (I remember thinking

A SURVIVAL GUIDE

they couldn't be serious—it was a joke. But they weren't kidding, were they?)

For a while I even thought it might be The Government (whoever it is)—but then I found the truth.

It was all of the above.

In a virtual war of money demands, we were living in a battlefield of ever-increasing poverty. And it was hard to find a place to duck.

At first we tried to make it. Some publishers' checks were still coming in, and Ruth, my wife, sold a painting now and then. And we got help from relatives, odd jobs, anything and everything that would support life and bring in a few dollars. We tried to be fair-play-Freddies and play by their rules.

I even wrote letters to the computers, trying to explain our plight and work things out. And the computers would answer, at first with a kind of mechanical compassion (Dear Friend: Perhaps you are having a temporary setback in your financial affairs?).

But in the end the computers wanted one thing and one thing only: Money. And in the end we had less and less of that same money. Clearly things couldn't continue in such and way and finally it came to a head.

There came a month when we had to make a choice between making that critical payment on the stereo (with tape deck and AM/FM and nice brushed metal surface), or filling the tank on one of the Pintos for a last wild ride into town to try to find part-time work. (Incidentally, it cost two dollars more to fill the tank then to make the stereo payment.)

We chose the gas and the man came to take the stereo. (About these men who came to take things: they all seemed to have come from the same mother. Each was pale, slightly overweight, and wheedled that he was, ". . . just doing my job.") From that point on, the loss of the stereo, it was a straight downhill shot, accelerating as we hit the steep parts that were greased.

We bought propane for heat and the man came to take the first Pinto. (Same man as with the stereo. I asked him about the stereo, but he told me not to make trouble so I didn't push it.) On this first car repossession I actually tried to reason with him, the man who came, by explaining that I had to buy propane or freeze. But he archly told me that I should have thought of that before I bought the car. When I pointed out that propane had gone up 640 percent since I bought the car he didn't hear me, so I didn't push it. (It marked the last time I ever tried to reason with the people who came to take things. My wife tried twice more and it nearly gave her a nervous tic—I actually think it did, but she insisted it was a temporary periodic squint and I can't argue with her.)

We filled the propane tank again two months later (it was a vicious winter) and the second car went. At this point I borrowed an ancient

A SURVIVAL GUIDE

Chevy pickup (1951 vintage) from a friend and that became our transportation.

As an aside: At this point we still, I believe, had thoughts of playing the game squarely. There was a significant amount of money due from a publisher and it would have been enough to square some of the rest of the debts (sailboat, personal notes, etc.). I remember sitting down and talking it over with my wife (that's what everybody says you should do—sit down and talk it over—but it doesn't make money come). We honestly decided that we could still make it. I think the phrase we used was "turn it around" before we lost it all.

Of course, we didn't know that oil was going up again, that interest rates were going to climb again, that it was all waiting to trip us up again, and that after a very brief respite—weeks, maybe a couple of months—we found ourselves two house payments down. Rather than face losing our equity, we sold the house and took the small profit out to our eighty acres where we intended to build our own home and live sans house payments.

We began to build—digging the foundation out by hand, using a mixer for the foundation cement—and I think we probably would have made it. The publisher hadn't sent the check, but he was promising to do so (he still hasn't); still, I thought it was all going to work out. The outstanding personal notes were all hanging fire (there was nothing left to take), and the small-farm bank was genuinely trying to work with us on the problems.

Then came the long gray car with the two men from the land-use commission. They came onto our land there in Colorado, got out of the car, and walked up to us; one of them—a thin man with an immense silver buckle and lots of silver and turquoise jewelry—stopped by the foundation.

"You can't be here," he said, with no preamble, no talk.

"I beg your pardon?" I said.

"You can't be here," he repeated, smiling.

"But this is my land. I own—will own it."

"Let me put it this way," he said, stepping down into the foundation. "You can be here but you can't be here. Do you understand?"

That was when my wife tried to reason with *Them*—the last time that brought on the temporary periodic squint. She talked until the edge of the rage came through, then wisely stopped. Murder would solve nothing. Well, almost nothing.

It seemed that though our driveway was a mile long, though the nearest neighbor lived several miles away, we couldn't stay on our land while we built our house—in spite of the fact that we had borrowed a modern camping trailer from a friend and that it had chemical toilets.

"You could stay in a motel in town and come out on weekends," the land-use man told us.

"That would be all right. But you can't be here."

Well. I did some quick figuring and found that if we stayed in a motel I would run up something close to the Kansas state debt. I finally, totally, completely admitted at that time that I was whipped. I could do no more. With no house, no money, no credit—I was poor.

More than poor, I was poor and no longer allowed in the system, in the machine—I was being shuffled out of the device the way a bent, folded, mutilated card is shuffled out of a computer. I was really whipped. And Ruth (I found later) came to the same feelings at the same time.

We left it then, the world of money and need. We left it not having made choice, but nearly having been driven away; we left it reluctantly, with a certain feeling of failure and depression. And if anybody had told me then that it was the best thing that ever happened to me I would have pummeled him. If somebody had said it would allow me to enhance the quality of my life, to live better, to enjoy my life more, I would have laughed in his face.

Yet it *was* the best thing that ever happened to me. And there is more quality, much more, than I ever thought my life would have—not to mention happiness and a measure of joy.

That was three years ago, as this is written. Three years of living outside the madness of the monetary system—three years of being poor, or having to exist in a money-oriented world with almost no money.

This book is about those three years, and in a very real way it might be termed a how-to guide for anybody who finds himself or herself suddenly on the raw edge of becoming poor—how-to not just make it, but actually improve your existence. (I know how that sounds, and it would have sounded the same way to me, but it's true. It's not only possible, but downright easy.)

But more than being just a guide, I hope this book will show in some degree how it is possible to take one step backward and come out about four steps ahead.

1

CHANGING YOUR THINKING

"In the final analysis it must be remembered that the turtle didn't lose. The turtle won the goddam race."

When the true realization that you've become poor hits you, the shock can be deadening. Reactions come something like the reactions of a chicken newly decapitated.

If it isn't panic it's something close to it. The reason—at least with us—was that our self-worth had become intricately interwoven with our capacity to make bucks. If we weren't smashing successes as shown by our bank balance and our ability to pay ever-greedier creditors (how can they *justify* the interest rates?), then we were less than what we could be. We were subpotential.

It was crushing. But just at first.

Just at the start was there an overwhelming feeling of despair and depression. No Mercedes.

BEAT THE SYSTEM

No Acapulco. No wild parties with the jet set in Monaco or skiing in Aspen or making love in the black sands of Tahiti.

All of it was gone. That was the feeling that came to us when we first honestly accepted being poor. Under-incomed. In tragic straits. Below norm, economically speaking.

Oh, there had been nudges of the feeling throughout the downgrading process—when the computers started barfing out the really nasty notices about taking your first-born son if you don't pay, or how their lawyers were going to take back your dental work if you didn't cough up. But we hadn't really accepted it yet.

And when we did, there was first the panic, then the depression—the knowledge that we probably wouldn't be rich. This was followed by three secondary reactions that are part of the restructuring process and are necessary to discuss as separate entities.

Breechclout Mentality

This was the back-to-nature syndrome, which took hold of me much stronger than it took my wife, who is basically urban while I am basically agricultural. In this thinking, which came right after the depression, the idea that one could run off into the brush and live life purely to live life was the predominant drive. I was ready for it and had even picked the place (somewhere east of Fairbanks). But Ruth had visions of eating things that came from under rocks and wearing animal skins and chewing leather to make clothing, so it was hard to sell the idea to her. I tried—even read parts of *Walden* to her—but it was no go. (Strangely, in an altered and sensible way, that is exactly what we wound up doing. But more of that later.) It's best to hold back on the breechclout thinking at first, but keep the thought handy because it is the kind of self-preservative thinking that is needed so much when the panic and initial reactions wear off.

The Julie Andrews Pick-Myself-Up-and-Start-Over-Again Mentality

Not that Julie has such a mentality, but many of her roles seem to be concerned with somebody who makes it, falls, and steps up to make it again. Like that ant and the rubber tree plant.

Well, if the truth were known, the banks probably wrote the song about the ant and the rubber plant. It is exactly what they want you to do, and to be honest, that feeling took hold of us right after we'd given up on breechclouts and skins. We dusted ourselves off, looked around, rolled up our sleeves, and prepared to do the whole business all over again. And to be truthful, I'm not sure what stopped us. But thankfully, something did because we were getting ready to repeat everything—including the disastrous mistakes. We could both work, go to regular jobs, rake in the bucks, get caught up, and start all over—that's the kind of thinking that caught us.

And with that kind of thinking came the concept of spending. It was a kind of madness. If we went out and got jobs and earned the money and got going again we could spend and spend and spend . . . the way an alcoholic drinks. (That's what my wife compared it to, and it's about right.)

This feeling was exceptionally powerful, lasted some days, and only the job scarcity probably kept it from taking over our lives. As it was, I did several résumés and circulated them around and—bless all personnel departments—I'm *still* getting answers from them after all these years up here in the north woods.

The I'm-a-Piece-of-Filth-Despair-Thinking

This form of poverty symptom came as soon as we genuinely realized that we couldn't tip over the rubber tree plant, and quite some time before we began to realize that ants aren't *supposed* to tip over rubber tree plants. Indeed, the whole concept of ants tipping over rubber tree plants was probably a function of somebody

A SURVIVAL GUIDE

trying to find a new way of harvesting rubber. Or trees. Or plants. Or ways to kill ants.

The depression was complicated and initially pushed us toward welfare and food stamps, living abjectly and pretty much hating everything west of St. Louis. Only our incredible disgust for anything to do with the system (after the land-use people were finished with us, the system became the enemy) kept us from complying with this despair-drive. We didn't do the stamps or the welfare or get involved with all the social-reform people then and still haven't. We have found, in all honesty, that they are basically worthless for anything practical. The bother of allowing them in your life—and it is a thorny bother—precludes any help they might ultimately give. You might pick up a few groceries, but the groceries are for the most part unhealthy to eat. And any direct financial aid you might get costs so much in integrity that it becomes crushingly demeaning to take it.

But the feeling of despair at first drove us there, or drove us that way. Again, only luck kept us from succumbing—luck and a kind of protective instinct that still follows us and has gotten stronger all the time.

In the end, or at least the end of the beginning, we did nothing.

For a few weeks we went nowhere, bought nothing but absolutely necessary food (meat and potatoes), using some of the very little money we had left from the sale of the house (dwindling now to almost nothing)—and we spent a lot of time trying to figure out what was happening to us.

We had become poor, that much we knew, but we weren't sure what it meant. After the first three syndromes wore off, the meaning of being poor was even more elusive. It surely didn't confine itself to the more or less socially acceptable meaning of poverty (that we were subhumans of some kind or other), and in this interim of doing nothing a strange thing happened.

Our values changed.

It was partly necessity, of course, but aside from being pushed into the change in value base there was a logic emerging—a logic and horror at what we had become.

By doing nothing—and I heartily recommend just this action for somebody newly poor—there was time to formulate thought about our actions and what evolved was pretty scary.

Before becoming poor we had become insane. Of course, the whole economic system had become insane as well—interest rates climbing like rockets, inflation nudging a true 20 percent (for the things we bought), income decreasing (through publishers' reluctance to send checks)—but that was no reason for us to go along with it. And yet we did. We borrowed more and more money—in fact through banks, and in essence through credit cards—and be-

A SURVIVAL GUIDE

came more and more a part of the problem until it completely dominated our lives.

Doing nothing gave us time and a way to see what we had become, and kept us from going back into the whole mess again. And when (it is, I suppose, no longer necessary to use the word *if*) becoming poor hits you, take that first step and do nothing.

Don't answer poison mail from creditors, don't talk to anybody but people you love, don't pay *any* bills to anybody, and don't buy a single thing that you don't truly and honestly have to have to support the basic necessities of life. Period.

Just stop and think. It is time to restructure, and that first stage of inactivity can give you time to gain strength and composure for the coming work. It will also start the necessary change of mental habits by introducing you to the first rule of being poor: don't ever buy anything. Not with money.

From this point on, the whole art of surviving and doing well as somebody who is poor depends on your ability to function either without money or at a very low money level. So at first, no matter what, try not to buy anything. From anybody.

On this business of restructuring—it is, naturally, mostly a mental change. And we found it

BEAT THE SYSTEM

a great help to think in terms of *Us* and *Them*, *We* and *They*.

We are the normal people, the people trying to survive in a world gone economically mad. *They* are the banks, oil companies, conglomerates, and big stores who are blatantly controlling the market and ramming the prices to us. *They* are the enemy, and when you start seriously considering the restructuring demanded by being poor, you find that all the bellowing about how bad it is to be poor comes from *Them*.

They have almost literally forced us into believing that being poor—even slightly poor—makes us undesirable. If it's Bigger and Shinier and Faster and More Modern and Cleaner and Higher and Wider and Longer and Leaner and Drier and Prettier and Slicker and Louder and Milder and Smoother and we don't have it, we're nothing.

That's what they would have us believe, that's the (pardon the expression) hype that they pump out continually, and that's the basic thought-force behind the concept that being poor (and not being able to have it all) is of necessity something distasteful.

In reality, the truth is exactly the opposite. As Thoreau pointed out (and it still holds), all of those things constitute a velvet-lined trap. It is the need to acquire and be affluent that makes one truly poor—not just in spirit (as it did with us), but in financial means as well. It was the insane push to acquire and own everything new and ostensibly better that drove us into poverty in the first place—so why shouldn't that same push now be considered as the villain?

When we realized that being poor was in truth another form of the expression of freedom, as it has turned out for us, it was as if a great weight were lifted from our shoulders. (That's dreadfully cliché, but it really was almost a lifting of a load.)

That was the primary move of our restructuring process: the simple but massive shift of thought from thinking poor was bad to seeing how good poverty could be. Of course, the terminology was more diverse—my wife thought of esoteric terms, almost spiritual terms, of how it was a true freedom of her human spirit. I—well, I thought of it as cutting through the crap. But the end result was the same.

The necessary, no, mandatory restructuring of thought had occurred. And if the immediate shock and pain had been seemingly severe, we found it much like having a bad tooth pulled: when it's out and gone, the relief is so overwhelming that it's nearly like being intoxicated. For a full week after we restructured and accepted and understood, we walked around smiling. Even the simple act of watching television became something of a pleasure.

"Look," Ruth said, during a commercial, "there's another piece of junk we don't have to buy."

BEAT THE SYSTEM

A truly marvelous feeling.

And one that sets the stage for the next, and more positive aspect of being poor—getting food and shelter, and keeping it once you've gotten it.

2
REALIGNING YOUR VALUE BASE

"See that skyscraper? That's just a place to store and move paper. That's all it is. And none of the paper means a goddamn thing. None of it is worth a tomato."

After the initial panic and restructuring has occurred there comes something my wife called the empty time. There isn't despair, exactly, although that feeling is slightly there. It's more just a time when there seems to be nothing happening. In a very real way it's like running a wasted race; like running a marathon that didn't mean anything and stopping in the middle. You feel as if you should be still running and yet you feel like stopping, too—just an empty place. A pausing place.

In our case the guilt came here, the true guilt of the whole situation. We had both been raised with strong Protestant work ethics and when there was not work and we no longer felt depressed, we felt guilty. We should be *doing* something, we felt—doing something right away. Working, slaving, making it; not to do those things felt wrong, made us guilty.

It was a time when we probably could have been swayed easily to climb back into the system and go downhill again, one of several times that came and sometimes still come. Then a wise man, a friend, took us aside and told us his maxim of life: Life genuinely demands only one thing of you, that you live it, and the corollary is to live the best way you know how.

That's all. No work ethic, no other true demands—not when you're getting down to basics. All that is needed is survival, is life, and everything else is secondary—at least initially.

It was then, and still is, a stunning concept for somebody rigidly brought up to think that if you didn't work, if you didn't contribute to the social structure and take your place and hold your place in that structure, you were less than nothing. It sounds so simple and yet is so difficult to utilize, to hold when being besieged from all sides by apparent information to the contrary.

It is *good* to achieve—that's the message crammed and screamed at us from the media. *Achieve* and *own* and *climb*—at the time of this writing the cliché phrase is "go for it."

And it is perhaps not altogether true to say that all those things are wrong except for one thing: They don't work. Taken objectively, the American—the international—concept of achieving basically sucks (as I saw written on a T-shirt) because what is achieved is so superficial. The average car won't last four years; the average suburban home won't make twenty years; a washer-dryer is used up in five years, if that. You work and work and buy and buy and at any given point if you compare what you're working for against what you're buying, you're a failure. What you get with the work isn't worth doing the work.

That pretty well blew the work ethic out of our tubes. All the things the ethic had gotten us, all the *things,* were worthless.

Still, there was that empty feeling. In my case it was noted primarily by an overpowering urge to do nothing, but to do it with great force and energy. On my wife's part there was a tendency to feel immensely frustrated.

It was a time when we found the first true course of action, the first positive approach to being poor. It was an action forced on us by our economic condition, but a good action nonetheless.

In the restructuring process it becomes mandatory to realign a usable value base. We sat in the small trailer on our land—they had given us a month to get off—and tried to decide what to do with the meager amount of money we had; what we could do with it to alleviate the problem.

"But that would involve spending it," Ruth pointed out. "And we don't want to spend it, do we?"

BEAT THE SYSTEM

Exactly. We decided to try for an extended period of time—a month—not to buy anything. Of course, it would be necessary to purchase some things—prescription drugs, very fundamental food. But that's all. We did this for two reasons: We were, in the first place, literally nearly broke and second, it was necessary to find out what we truly had to have versus what we *thought* we had to have. There is a tremendous difference between these two items, a difference based almost entirely on the advertising industry and not on need. If you don't buy anything for a month, as truly little as you possibly can, some very striking things can happen to you—and did to us.

We underwent a withdrawal of such magnitude that I am still wondering what in hell happened. Or how it came to be.

When we started the Mad Month (as my wife termed it), we had on hand twenty pounds of potatos, three pounds of cheap hamburger, various assorted cans of soups and beans, a can of shortening, and four loaves of bread. Clearly not enough to feed three people (my son was six at the time) for a month. We also had one hundred and three dollars and forty-six cents.

We had a place to live, of a sorts, in the camping trailer and in that we were perhaps slightly ahead of the game. We would not have to scramble for a house or rent payment for at least a month—but more of that later.

We did not have coffee, or very little. I think

there might have been enough for two pots on hand, but it was at this time that coffee became so outrageously expensive so there was no possibility of buying more. This may have been part of the reason for the withdrawal symptoms, or it may have been the lack of sugar—there was absolutely no money for any kind of junk food or sweets. Nothing but basic food and damn little of that.

So we worked up a primary diet of meat and bread and potatoes and we used that for the month (we of course bought more potatoes and ground meat). And we hunkered in to see what happened.

For the first week there were a series of discoveries. It was simply awesome to find how much we live on that we honestly don't use or need. We had been heavy coffee drinkers and smokers (I smoked two packs a day), and I thought if you didn't have coffee and a cigarette in the morning your heart wouldn't start. I also laced my coffee liberally with sugar, and had I really paused to examine the way I lived and ate I would have made the average health-food addict die.

All of that came to a screeching halt that first week. Coffee ended the second day, ditto for the cigarettes; and without coffee and cigarettes there wasn't really much to put the sugar in. I picked up a copy of *The Good Earth* by Pearl Buck (highly recommended reading for the first two weeks of poverty) and while reading of the wretched condition of Wang Lung, I saw that he sometimes had hot water to drink in the morning. I tried this, with sugar and it didn't work for me. (My wife didn't try it, probably because her addiction to a morning drink wasn't as strong.)

Common initial symptoms were straightforward and strong enough to make my son want to leave home: We both became ogres. On the second morning I know my incisors were turning into fangs and I could easily have taken an ax and wiped out an entire community for a cup of coffee and a cigarette. Ruth and I studiously avoided each other, spoke only when we absolutely had to, and then in monosyllabic grunts; this tension and severity increased until I found myself sitting beneath a pine tree, wringing my hands and crying. (My wife, incidentally, experienced the same feeling at about the same time.) This was at the end of the third day and was followed on the fourth day by a lessening—a very notable lessening—of the physical torture of the symptoms and an increase in the mental strain. There was massive guilt, a total shaking of any kind of self-worth left based on external social values, and a final realization that we were truly poor. (This was not the grinding poverty we would experience later and have to deal with, but a mental attitude shift that I believe was the onset of a mental commitment to find something useful to do with the rest of our lives. It was that profound and basic.)

Physical symptoms for day four were light-headedness (almost a high), and a feeling of losing weight, even though we were eating meat and potatoes twice a day. Significantly, we had completely stopped eating any kind of in-between-meal food—no candy, no treats of any kind for the child except those we could make ourselves, like popcorn—and we actually did lose weight. I had been about thirty pounds overweight, my wife much less than that, and I think in that first week I perhaps lost three or four of those pounds. (I have since lost all of them.)

An important aside: Neither of us drink any intoxicating beverages or smoke anything that will alter the mind. So all the symptoms described are straight and not induced by chemicals, at least none we knew about. We were eating cheap ground meat and who knows what they had in that.

Sleepiness and lassitude were predominant in that first week, as were desires for THINGS. We kept a list of things we missed or wanted most and it is truthful to state that almost nothing on the list is worth having. Gloppy foods, for example, rich and thick and disgustingly fattening. On one occasion we went to a store to get more potatoes and meat and we nearly broke down passing the bakery section, and then again at the little candy rack by the cash register.

Cigarettes were on the list, and coffee, and pastry, and a house with conveniences, and more cigarettes and pastry and coffee and bread and steak (from my son). In the second week there came a shift in the list. There is a distinct break in the middle of the second week, when what is listed no longer is junky or base but starts to take on a realistic flavor. *Better* meat appears more often and other forms of staples—flour, salt, beans, fresh fruit and vegetables. Never potatoes, I might add, and they still don't appear on any want list. Never again potatoes.

In the second week two other things became predominant: All three of us were made slightly ill by Ads for thick-rich food on the television, and we began to enjoy a kind of physically uplifting feeling that is still very much in our lives.

I am not a nutritionist, and I know very little about which foods do what or how they do it. But there was an extremely strong tie between our diet and the way we felt. We had lived primarily on fast foods, not just from the junky burger stands but the kind that comes from the store—prefrozen chicken, bread, French-fried potatoes, that sort of thing. Quite a lot of candy, especially for the boy, and chips and dip, rich desserts—the same diet that I suppose prevails for most of the country.

When we left this diet and went to straight basic foods, after a period of a week or slightly more we noticed this lightening in our lives; almost a definite lifting feeling. We had much more energy and awakened feeling better. To

A SURVIVAL GUIDE

be sure a measure of this reaction was from the forced cessation of smoking, but we felt it also had a lot to do with the food.

It was the first instance, although we didn't see it at the time, of the illustration that poverty can be quite good for you if you have been excisting in the upper middle class.

We still keep the list from time to time, a running want list, especially when we begin to feel deprived by our seeming lack of material wealth. It puts things in the right perspective and pins down what is truly important in our lives. When you are living close, as Hemingway put it, living close and tight, and you write on a list that what you really want is a Ding-Dong or a new pair of jeans that cost forty dollars or a parakeet or a new car for seven or eight thousand—then look at the list a day or two later when that initial compulsion has left you. It can do wonders for your life. There is a kind of joy in knowing that you would have sold your soul for a Twinkie and chose not to.

During the month we had to buy more meat and potatoes. We stayed with cheap hamburger and the cheapest potatoes we could find. We also bought some green vegetables (lettuce, stringbeans, celery) and two cans of shortening and some salt and pepper. We did *not* buy chips, dip, canned meat or fish, pastry, bread (we had some flour on hand and made perhaps twelve loaves), cigarettes, coffee, tea, sugar, candy, cans of soup or beans or circle-shaped pizza cutters, though by the time we'd gotten through the supermarket and especially past the bakery section we dearly wanted all those things.

"I would sell my body for an eclair," my wife said as we whooshed through the automatic door and went to our old truck, dragging the boy behind us. "Twice."

It was not easy. But we did it, and at the end of the first month, when we had to leave our land and live with very little or no money we had learned a truth that still takes us through many a night.

We can live, live better and in a more healthful manner—speaking both physically and spiritually —without almost all the trappings of so-called progress. It is sad, perhaps tragic, but the truth is that nearly everything put forth by our culture as good and meaningful and worth having is worthless. Or, as my son put it: "How come everything they advertise on television breaks?"

On boredom—being poor can be a very boring situation. *Can* be, but needn't. There are many ways to alleviate the boredom, but there is some danger. If you choose to watch the tube, remember that on commercial televison you are being constantly bombarded with messages to buy various forms of unnecessary junk, much of it aimed at (a) your belly and (b) your self-worth image. Since becoming poor has drastically altered both your food intake and (probably) your image of self-worth, the commercials can be rather difficult to take—even more so than usual. We stopped watching commercial television (still don't watch it), and when we want that sort of entertainment we try public television. A secondary note: We also made love more, and as we lost weight and the general heaviness of fast and junk food left us, the quality of this expression against boredom improved dramatically. My son got into several craft hobbies, such as carving, using raw materials of his own making; some of the things he made during that time are still on display around the house. There is one owl that is particularly good and is also a handy reminder that it is much nicer than a plastic airplane model.

Basically, to stop the boredom we read—read voraciously. Below is a recommendation of books that helped.

The Good Earth, Pearl Buck

For those who may not have been exposed to this rare and wonderful book, it is about a Chinese man named Wang Lung, who starts in unbelievable poverty as a farmer and works his way through the pitfalls of success just prior to and during the Chinese Revolution. We reread this book periodically when we start to get down (less and less often) about not HAVING AND HAVING as we think of it. Wang Lung had nothing. Literally nothing. And to see that, to read that, somehow makes us feel better. Aside from a few cultural and economic differences there is very little disparity between us and Wang Lung: we want the same things. Life, happiness in some measure, food and warmth and a place to live.

The Trees, The Fields, Conrad Richter

These are novels about the early exploration and settling of the American wilderness. Aside from being fascinating reading—Mr. Richter's research is concise—they are informative from the standpoint of being poor in that they show how to live with nothing and find something to use within that framework. Some early American settlers would arrive in an area with only a saucepan and the clothes on their backs and would be envied because they had the saucepan. And they did not feel deprived.

A Moveable Feast, Ernest Hemingway

This nonfiction work about his early days in Paris is a very definite must book for the newly poor. Hemingway lived in stunning poverty then, but found beauty and joy. He wrote of it in such a way as to make poverty seem almost enjoyable. He makes being hungry a thing to be desired and at one point the simple act of having an orange becomes a reward of magnificent proportions.

There are of course many other books that will help you understand and adapt to being poor, but the above will provide a start. Don't buy them. Use the library—from this point on it will be necessary to use the very maximum of unpaid-for services, and the library is a good start.

A final note on adaption to poverty. At the end of a month, for us, it came down to two things. For the boy, it was a model. He'd wanted one and we used a small amount of the remaining fifty-odd dollars to buy him one. It broke a week after he'd completed it and he didn't notice that it was gone.

For my wife and me it came to two Snickers candy bars. We had been insatiable candy-bar eaters and Snickers was our favorite. It hit us as an incredible thing that we could go in one short month from lusting and wanting such things as yachts and color televisions and new cars down to one small candy bar. But that's what happened as we kept paring down the monthly list, cutting away the stuff we didn't really want to what we thought we wanted—it boiled down to one candy bar each. Snickers.

BEAT THE SYSTEM

And when the month was up we went to the shopping center—where, incidentally, it was much easier to pass displays without wanting to buy everything—and bought the boy a model and bought ourselves a candy bar each.

We couldn't eat them. At one time in our lives eating a Snickers bar took two or three minutes and was not noticeable; this time, however, we couldn't eat them. They are so rich, so, so *much* when you are used to not eating them and haven't eaten them in a month—haven't eaten anything rich or sugary—that we simply couldn't get them all down. After a bite, a small bite, we rewrapped them for later—they lasted four days—and got back in the truck. It is perhaps not quite correct to say that we felt pride, but it was something very close. We had no real place to live, just over fifty dollars to our name, and were driving a truck nearly as old as we were. Yet there was something of triumph in not being able to get that Snickers bar down, some new feeling of what we had become and would yet become.

"Why am I happy?" my wife asked as she put her Snickers in her purse. "I shouldn't be happy."

"I know. I feel the same way."

We still feel happy.

3

GETTING SOME MONEY

> "If you have enough money you can do anything. Anything. Or if you don't have enough money you can do anything. There are always two choices."

When the initial changing period is over—well, not over since it goes on and on—and when you have made the move from middle class to poor in your mind, there seems to come a whole raft of things and thoughts that have to be acted upon and considered at the same time.

You'll need a place to live, more food, some money to buy the food (no matter how little or where it comes from, you need some money), clothing (it all seems to wear out when you get poor—instantly), car parts (it will break down as soon as you can't afford to fix it, Hemstead's law so states), and on and on.

It can be an overwhelming experience if allowed to run unchecked, but the solution is simple; just take them one at a time, doing the most critical first.

BEAT THE SYSTEM

Food and money to buy it are first priorities on the list, and bring you in initial contact with the government. There are funds available to help people who are suddenly poor, funds for food and rent or house payments, and funding is something you perhaps should look into.

I say perhaps because it was very difficult for us to do this—in fact, we still haven't. I don't know why. Certainly it's not an ethical matter. We paid into the government who knows how many thousands and thousands of dollars in one form of tax or another and taking some of it back out would only be fair. But we just haven't been able to bring ourselves to allow the system into our lives in that way. It is, however, a very personal matter and shouldn't negate the services offered by various government agencies.

As a point in fact what we did, for steady money coming in, was a use of government funds. It was just not in the social context. I went back to college—I was, at the time, just under forty—because I found that I could still use some of my GI money available. It brought in nearly four hundred a month and though a goodly portion of this amount went to the college, there was still just over two hundred a month to use for other things. A house or rent payment, to be specific. I only qualified for veteran's money for about seven months, but it was some money coming in for those seven months while we figured out what to do and where to go.

A SURVIVAL GUIDE

I took minimal, easy courses (I say this without blushing because after nearly four years in the army I've got *something* coming) with a lot of home study and did only enough work to get by. I then took a part-time job in construction, doing roof repair and remodeling, and that brought in another three hundred, averaged out, so we were right back up to about five. Somehow we always seem to be able to live on that kind of money—at least living poor, as we now were. Of course, when we did two car payments, the house payment, the boat payment the stereo payment, the freezer payment, the washer-dryer payment, the sporting goods payment, the utilities payments, etc., it was a slightly different matter—then we needed just under two grand a month to get by.

The main concept of this money thing is to go at it from as many different angles as you can. Later in the book there will be a section on how to live on nearly nothing when that rare occasion occurs and there is just simply no money to get anywhere.

But usually there is a way to get some funding, or many ways. Attack them all. The primary drive that comes with poverty is to seek money until you get very hungry or thirsty, and then it's food and water.

Try food stamps if you qualify. Try welfare (or whatever they call it in your area). Try fuel aid or air conditioning aid and college money or home-study grants or anything you can to get some money coming in. Try them all. Have a yard sale or rummage sale, especially if you are leaving your house. Look for all forms of work and do them all, even those you think might be too menial. Take all the money from all the sources, any and *all* of it, and rathole it. Don't spend any of it on anything but food and shelter. Let them have the cars and stereos and the rest of it because if you try to save all of those things you will drive yourself back down into the pit again.

And since going down into that pit is probably what got you poor in the first place, or at least was a major contributing factor, why do it again?

The basic thing with this money business, the only thing thing that's really important, is not to limit yourself. No amount is too small to get, and no legal method too demeaning—including a few that are on the edge of being slightly wrong, as far as that goes.

We made the initial mistake of still thinking in terms of being upper middle class and when I had a chance to do a half day of work or something along that line I would pass it up as not being worth the bother. That was incorrect, to say the least. But at first we didn't understand the tremendous change in attitude we would get concerning money.

We had been caught up in the glut that was and is sweeping the country. Perhaps the best illustration of how insane this is comes with the knowledge that we live in the only country in the world where they are making a kind of bread out of wood so that people can continue to gorge themselves without getting fat.

It is not a pretty thing to think about. It is even less pretty when you think of yourself in these terms. And yet that's what we were; we were caught in the glut syndrome and I'm sure in a very short time would have had to eat the wooden bread (Heaven knows we qualified).

We had to have more. Always more of whatever it was we were doing or had at the moment. If more money came in—rare, but it happened—we would have to spend it on acquiring more. Just more.

Consequently, our feelings about money were altered by our tendency to glut. There was never enough, not even when we got a lot. Because what we *wanted,* the glut, moved just ahead of what we could ever get in. It was an endless race and we were losing.

It was sad. I would sell a book, get a decent advance, and it was spent before I truly got it—just on bills and getting more of whatever it was we were glutting on at the moment. Always broke, always moving one step behind (until we went down)—the money that came in was never enough. It wasn't worth having. Or doing.

And this feeling, this why-bother-if-it-just-isn't-a-huge amount feeling, bled over into our new-poor existence. I wouldn't do a small job because the money wasn't worth the work.

BEAT THE SYSTEM

But it came to be. In a very short time, three months at the outside, our whole approach to money—how we dealt with it and felt about it—altered dramatically. I suppose you could call it part of the withdrawal from being middle class, although we didn't think of it that way at the time.

What happened is that without all the payments, without the glut going on, the money that came in could actually *buy* something. It was incredible. It still is. After they repossess (what a marvelous word, that, to possess again), they can't have any more money. That's a rule. Of course they can sue, as we had one bank do to us, and make it a civil matter, but they can't have the money you would have had to pay for the unit if they take back the unit, whether it be car, stereo, boat, or television. (There will be a section shortly on legal problems.)

The point is that when all that money wasn't going out for junk we found that we had money for valid stuff—food, good food, became something we bought often. Our true paradox of poverty (to coin a phrase) is that becoming poor allowed us to eat butter. Real butter. When we had money and were part of the middle class we had to eat margarine.

The money we got in, admittedly smaller amounts, went a lot farther. It didn't go out on car payments and the like and because of that our attitude towards that money, towards our lives, changed.

A SURVIVAL GUIDE

At first, with the money we lost the feeling of glut. Then it moved to other aspects of our life (eating, for instance). After a time I was taking any and all jobs and when I'd get thirty or forty dollars it was as if I'd gotten five thousand when we were living supposedly high off the hog. Two hundred, three hundred became amounts of significance, truly large amounts of money, even with the madness of inflation—and they still are. The way we now live, if we get two hundred dollars it means at least twenty times what two thousand used to mean.

So work at the attitude shift. We made the mistake of waiting until it came naturally. If you can make it happen you'll be better off. Then when you get money—any way you can—it will mean something.

Being poor gives you tremendous power, probably a lot more power than being truly rich. We did not understand this, either, at first and spent a lot of time working on our self-worth image when we were forced to deal with creditors and the like from a legal angle. We felt as if they were right, as if they had all the cards, and as if they could do anything they wanted. Actually, in all three areas it was exactly the opposite. Because we were poor we had been given power we did not understand. It is the same power that a wild animal has when it cornered, its back against the wall—and it is truly formidable.

BEAT THE SYSTEM

Being poor, as already discussed, seems to be made up largely of paradoxes. Probably the most ridiculous of these paradoxes is the fact that the first thing that seems to happen when you get poor and run out of money is that everybody *wants* money. There is, of course, very much the feeling of rats leaving a sinking ship about all of this, and taken in that light it is rather humorous.

We experienced this ridiculous feeling of impishness about it all. There we were, one little family with no money, nothing really coming in, and here were all these megacorporations, huge banks full of literally uncountable amounts of money. And they were all screaming in effect that they would collapse and that we would turn into subhumans if we didn't find some money for them right away—when, if we *had* been able to find some money it all wouldn't have happened in the first place. It's ridiculous.

But the point is that when the money stops coming in and hence going out, they start to scream and that's the way to look at it—as simple screaming. They use a legalese format for their screams, and they use collection agencies and lawyers and perhaps even the courts, but it is still only screaming and as such essentially ineffective.

They are allowed to take back whatever it was you used the money to borrow, as in stereo, car, etc. But that's it. Give those things back and you're done. The best way to handle the whole thing with the creditors is to keep a low, very cool profile.

The *very* best thing is to do nothing. Period. Don't answer their mail, don't talk to them. When they call tell them your foot is bleeding (I actually used that once) and hang up. Any contact with them is bad for you and good for them. Just let them come and get their junk back (look at it that way—not as MY STEREO, but as their junk), although you don't have to actually "let" them do anything, but can force them to work at it a bit and be done with it.

Don't write them any letters (that's worth repeating) and no matter what they say or do, DON'T SIGN ANYTHING! They like to have written things in their files from you, things they can use as leverage, and it must be denied them. They get their junk back, but that's all.

When you become poor you become powerful. You have nothing more to lose and from that position it's hard to lose, really. When they realize that you're going to fight, that all they can do is spend more money through their lawyers and get nothing out of you, they will back off. Banks are nothing if not pragmatic.

It is just a matter of knowing how to use that power and how to remain strong and let them wear out.

DON'T SIGN ANYTHING! (One more time.)

BEAT THE SYSTEM

About getting lawyers—they are of dubious help other than to ease your mind a bit. It is possible that they could help if you had some money and were trying to hang onto it, but since you have none there is not much that a lawyer can do for you.

And the first time you get a bill from one of them and see such things as, "Fifteen minutes of telephone conversation with client—$15.00," it makes you wonder if they're ever any good. We tried one and it cost more than we would have saved, although we did get a little peace of mind—at least until we got the bill from him.

One thing of vital importance: saving your home. Assuming you have some kind of money available (welfare, aid, odd jobs, however it can be gotten), and you own or are buying a home, you may wish to save it. The word *may* is used because there will be other alternatives discussed later.

They will try to get it because it represents money to them. They can sell it and take the money. So it is necessary to save it, literally, if you want to keep it.

In this event you might wish to get a lawyer to see if it can be protected. We have since bought a place—although not truly a home when we bought it, but some woods—and have made sure it is protected.

Many states (where we live now, for instance) have laws protecting the homestead, making it exempt from legal action or judgments. We did not know this until we got a lawyer who explained it to us, and in that sense a lawyer might be called useful. The same information can be gotten free, however, by calling the county attorney and asking.

If you are buying your own place and such a law is applicable, by all means file your house as a homestead—this works for urban situations as well—and make it as safe as possible. Often there are also exempt a certain amount of personal goods for the running of your life—in our case, up to three thousand dollars worth—and that is worth checking as well. Leave no stone unturned, as they say, but remember never to get into a litigative situation if it can possibly be avoided.

Any and all contacts with lawyers should be kept as brief, in minutes, as possible. They cost way too much and give you way too little for them to be worthwhile. And if you get into a lengthy court situation, you'll probably wind up with the same initial debt plus a whopping attorney fee on top. You can't beat them except to avoid them completely.

A last thought on all this debt hassle, something that hit us hard. When they start coming at you from all sides—and they will, like sharks on what they think is a fresh kill—they have absolutely no scruples. One man from a finance company we had used to buy the stereo called my wife's mother and told her there had "been an accident and we had some insurance problems that would need money." I can't say the name of the company without getting sued, except it wasn't a fly-by-night business but was a large national concern.

The primary thing is that they will do anything to get money. They are filthy about it, to be blunt, and one of the things they do is try to destroy your ego. The reason for this is basic—to give them psychological advantage. And when they have that advantage they can pressure you and lean on you to find money for them—money that you need to live yourself.

For that reason all those letters, even the ones the computers write, come at you like personal attacks. And when they call—if you still have a phone—they speak in terms of your worth, your credit, and how it's tied to your value as a citizen, as a human being, as a grown, mature, responsible individual.

They make it all not just a financial setback, which it is, but a personal tragedy that they claim will ruin your life through ruining your credit—which in our case we would have been much better off to avoid in the first place.

It can be a pretty devastating attack because it is so vicious and comes from so many different angles at once. Lawyers, collection agencies, bankers, and secretaries from all of the above seem to be chewing at you all the time and when you couple the multipronged assault with the fact that you are truly poor and having

A SURVIVAL GUIDE

trouble making it anyway, it can be nearly overwhelming.

When it got really bad for us and the attacks were coming at their worst we began to fight and that was the only really bad part. We started to take it out on each other, arguing and blaming. Of course, that was wrong, wrong and frightening. I'm not sure when we realized that we were fighting about nothing but we did; in the midst of arguing we smiled, and it hit both of us in the same time that it was useless to argue about money for all the people who were demanding it because it just wasn't there.

After that it became a game. *Us* against *Them.* And the striking part of it was that in the end we won. We didn't get the money to pay them, our credit with the big national credit corporations is lousy (thank goodness), but we won. We no longer live with the hammer of payments over our heads, we no longer buy what we cannot afford, we no longer glut. They still do, and do it on such a scale that it is a little hard to believe.

When it was really bad and I started to believe them about how my worth really was tied up to my credit—my ability to buy what I could not afford—when it really got bad and we were fighting each other and there was nothing but bad taste in our mouths all the time, when it got that bad . . . one morning when I opened the mail and got the usual poison from the collection agencies, the thought struck me from the

BEAT THE SYSTEM

blue that if I had simply invented the bobby pin none of this would be.

All that money.

I do not know why this silly thought made me feel better but it did, brought everything into perspective.

What we finally boiled down out of all this stew of garbage were three powerfully important priorities concerning all future use of money.

First, food and clothing and welfare for ourselves. *They*—the big companies—truly don't give a damn for you as a human being, so you must.

Second, shelter. (covered in the next chapter.) And it must be adequate, not a tent (unless you want one) or old piano crate in back of the department store. Good housing, decent housing.

Third, if there's any money left over it should perhaps be applied to bills, but only if you're sure the money isn't going to be needed in the near future for the first two priorities. It sounds horribly selfish and self-centered, but we found that it has to be that way. If we accepted any undue hardship to make the banks happy we discovered that our own plight went downhill so fast that recovery was extremely difficult. And if we couldn't recover there was no hope of ever paying off the bills.

Sometimes, for some people, it is desirable to pay off whatever bills they can, especially when they are local bills or bills owed to acquaintances—special bills. We had several such debts and they had to be paid. One was the local small grocer who had extended us credit for food when there was not another way to eat. He could not have absorbed too many losses. Another was a man who sold firewood locally. We had to pay bills of this nature but we also found that we couldn't pay them off totally for a long time. In this case, we went to the people and told them the truth—that we were poverty stricken, that we hadn't planned it, that we would try to pay them off but that it would take some time.

The truth is a good policy in all instances except when talking to lawyers and politicians—then say nothing. They don't believe you anyway.

A quick list of what was easy and what was not so easy for us to do without.

Things We Didn't Miss At All

Bills. (The long term kind—five year, etc.)
Telephone. (Think on it—when's the last time that miserable beast brought you *good* news?)
Car insurance. (More on this later in the car chapter.)
Coffee. (I know, hard to believe. But it is really amazingly easy to quit drinking the stuff. Try it.)

Television. (It was so awful when we lost the set, but when we quit watching it was an actual relief.)

All credit cards.

Continuing credit accounts. (These tore us apart—you can charge so much in such a short time.)

Junk food. (First few days were hard, then it became very easy.)

Outside entertainment. (Most films are on a television level anyway, or lower.)

Repair bills. (You really *can* do it all yourself. More on this later.)

Things We Missed

Cigarettes. (Although the feeling is totally gone now and it's wonderful not to smoke, it was hard to stop.)

I started this list with all intentions of explaining what it was hard for us to live without and we sat and stared at each other and honestly can't come up without anything other than cigarettes and that only on a very temporary basis. The truth is that we don't miss much of anything about that other life we lived. There was some missing when we first left it, but it was all so superficial and general that perhaps it might be just as well to say that at first we missed the so-called convenience and let it go at that. Nor is this a gimmick—we actually don't miss any of what we were. It's astounding when it hits you that way; years and years we busted our tails to make it, to make something that we couldn't even understand, and now we sit and stare at each other and try to remember what we missed about all of that and nothing comes.

You'd think there would be something, wouldn't you?

4

LIVING SPACE

> "The old one about if you're so smart why aren't you rich doesn't scan. If it did I would be dead and Rockefeller would be alive."

You can, of course, live anywhere, if you have to. But the whole idea of accepting being poor and living with higher quality almost demands that you come up with housing that is not just survival oriented but of some acceptable order, something you can like.

First, however, some words on that business of survival—a discussion of ifs.

If you are in dire straits, if you must leave where you are living and have no place else to go immediately, if it all seems to be falling apart on you—remember, you can live *anywhere* for a time.

It is something we seem to forget. We have taken ourselves so seriously that we have forgotten how we started, and how we are not so very far from there now. Speaking in terms of housing we have removed ourselves from simplicity and have gone to such a complicated state of affairs that housing has become a nightmare—a nightmare so expensive that it's insane.

In truth, housing means simply a place to live, a place to be. And all the other stuff, the extras like furniture and garbage disposals and lights and even heat—all of that is secondary to the concept of shelter. A roof that will keep moisture out and provide shelter—that's housing, speaking historically, or prehistorically. Everything else came later.

If you are between the rock and the hard place it is a good thing to remember.

In the terms of being poor the concept of housing can be broken down into the following areas:

Survival

Actually, from research and from our own case, this first category seems to be very common. Raw, wide open, brutal survival—many people suddenly find themselves without a place to live. Their money is gone and the mortgage holder comes for the house, or they are to be evicted from where they live for nonpayment of rent. In our case we were simply told by the state that we could not live on our own land. Incredible.

A SURVIVAL GUIDE

So first, absolutely first, remember the priorities—take care of you and yours. It isn't necessary to do anything to be nice to people who are foreclosing or kicking you out. While it is true that in the end they have the law on their side, you are not without recourse. Not too long before this was written, a situation erupted that illustrates how far survival can be carried.

Not too far from where we now live a couple rented a small trailer. They paid the first month's rent, or the state did, since they were on welfare. Then the state apparently decided they did not qualify for welfare and made no further payments. The couple made no further payments either, but they lived there, rent free, for twelve *months*. It took the landlord that long to get them out legally. It was bitter and acrimonious, and the lawyers were having a field day. In the end the landlord was to be pitied because the couple virtually demolished the trailer and ruined the place. But the fact is that through hook and crook, by claw and nail they managed to live there for a year without making any rent payments.

They survived.

And that is the key to the first approach to housing. If you are in a position of having to survive, you make every shot count. Don't give them a thing. Don't move out unless and until you absolutely have to, legally. Period. *Make* them move you out. And all the while they are moving you, keep looking for a place to land, a place to live.

In that respect you have a lot of options. We had friends who found one of those largish army surplus tents—the kind that sleep ten men—and spent an idyllic summer in Jackson Hole, Wyoming, camping in the high country. Another couple we met during research found some land for no money down and twenty dollars a month in New Mexico and built an adobe hut that actually turned out rather nice. They still have that payment of course, but twenty a month for a house payment isn't bad. They had been paying close to a thousand, and most of that was interest. In our case we went to the north woods and built a place. But that doesn't mean going back to the land is the only way.

When you are surviving you can find places to live in the city as well. Perhaps a classic illustration of this is one couple in Los Angeles we talked to about housing. They were very poor. He'd been an aerospace engineer when the bottom dropped out of that technology (although it's coming back now), and they lost everything, including their house. They had no children, which made it a little easier, but the form of housing they found is interesting. They never live in one place for more than one or two months. What happened is that about when they got evicted they had some friends who were decidedly not poor and who were going on an extended vacation in Europe. It seems these friends needed somebody to house-sit watch their place, while they were gone. Word has a way of getting around and in no time they were house-sitting another place, then another, and now they are booked ahead two *years* for people who are leaving their homes for a time. Two years of living in rather nice homes with no payments of any kind, including utilities, and no chance to get bored with where they are living. True, they haven't got a true home—but then they have none of the attendant headaches of home owning, either. All they have to worry about is a bit of food and some clothing. They don't own a car, ride bikes (which you can get away with in Los Angeles if you don't have to do that freeway shuffle for miles and miles) when they need to go somewhere, and live a kind of perpetual vacation.

The height of this sitting business is a single young woman we interviewed who was a caretaker for yachts. She lived on one sailboat after another and made sure they weren't ripped off. She was another casualty of the aerospace business in southern California.

These are forms of survival housing that show best the concept that you needn't go through undue hardship to survive.

You can, however, lower your standards a bit. If, for instance, you have children it's a good bet you're not going to be baby-sitting yachts. Same goes for pets. In that case there are many other ways to approach the problem.

BEAT THE SYSTEM

Look for a small, older house trailer. They can be awfully cheap and you can sometimes work a deal for nothing down and small payments, even when you haven't got any credit. Then find a place to park it—not a trailer park, but check with anybody with an open area of land: farmers, future construction sites, that sort of thing. True, trailers—old ones—can be a pretty ragged way to live; small, cramped, and unpleasant. But we're talking survival here and we found it wasn't so bad if we came at it like boat living. A place for everything and everything in its place, keep everything clean and put away, spend a lot of time on "outside" living—we sat outside every chance we got, used the trailer for sleeping and shelter when it rained—and understand and accept that it's just a temporary form until you can find a better way to live. (Note: We are not talking now about those travel trailers in which many retired folks live all the time, all around the country. That costs money, is definitely a luxury form of easy living, and shouldn't be attempted unless you've got the trailer and the rig to pull it free and clear, in which event you're probably not poor and can afford the horrendous gasoline prices for pulling one of those things around.)

Look for an apartment that needs a manager, which will defray the payment at least in part, or perhaps whole. Or try to find an apartment complex or retirement center that needs a maintenence person. In the end, don't forget that what you're trying to do is get by. If you happen to fall into a situation that proves nice or permanent, go ahead and accept it.

But don't forget the tent. Or, as one couple we know did, live in your car. They had an older station wagon and when nothing else presented itself they put all their possessions in a friend's garage and slept in the back of their car for a few weeks, cleaning up at gas stations, until they found an old house to fix up.

Which leads to the next category of housing, something a bit more solid.

A Place To Live

Once you have found a place to survive, a place that gives you time to look around and find something better—if, indeed, you don't see something good at first—you will need a place to live while you are learning the ropes of being poor. We are still not talking about what you will be doing or where you will be living for the rest of your life, but a secondary temporary form. Perhaps a house. Somewhere for a year or so while you look and think and plan, perhaps; a place to contemplate and live for a time.

A good idea in the vein is the old home that is in sad need of repair. There are examples all over the place and usually you can rent one dirt cheap or simply make your work fixing up the place your monthly payment. Try calling a realtor and asking if he knows of any such places you can fix up. They often know marginal places that would be marketable if they were fixed up and the two of you might work out a deal.

Abandoned homes, and there are surprising numbers of them, fall into this category. Just dig around until you find the owner or responsible person and explain how much nicer it would be to have somebody living in the place to keep it up, fix it up, etc. The owner winds up with a better place and you wind up with a place to live.

Flexibility is the rule in this area. Remember, you're looking for a place that is just a little less temporary than the survival level so it isn't necessary to get anything that solid. Of course, if it comes along, take it, but if not—beggars truly can't be too choosey.

If you're not locked into living in a city, check surrounding farms. Larger farms often have unused migrant farm housing (really) during the off months and while it usually isn't very nice it can be suitable for a time. Most of them don't mind giving you a place to stay to keep the places up a bit. (We once lived at an apple orchard in just this manner, in the migrant farm workers' housing. It wasn't bad.)

Stay loose. Move with the flow.

A Home

There are a whole bunch of variables and secondary factors in this section, and for that reason it is necessary to leave the actual subject for a bit.

Getting a home, a place to live permanently, a way to live, involves several commitments that many people decide not to make. We chose to live without the horrible monetary hammer over our heads all the time. Once driven poor by the system we talked it over—about four thousand times—and decided to go ahead and accept living poor, and to live that way from then on, a way we still live. But many will not want to make that step.

Many find that it's too difficult to live without the seeming ease and convenience of monetary living. Of course, a good case could be made—as we try to make it—that all of those so-called easy trappings are really so hard to get by working that they cost more (in cardiacs, stress, etc.) than they can possibly be worth. But still, many will have rebelled against poverty and get back, or want to get back into the system and start over, rebuild their lives and all that.

More power to them, and I wish them luck because they'll need it. The thing is if you decide to do that, this is the place to do it. If you are not going to accept living poor, then get back into the system before you start working on getting a home.

BEAT THE SYSTEM

The commitment to living in a home while poor is more than just looking for a cheap place. It demands a likewise commitment in the style that you choose to live as well—*demands* it—and if you decide to go back do it before you start to work on getting a home. Otherwise, there is a chance that you will try to bring some of the money ways of doing things into living poor and in that there is most definitely only destruction. The two won't mix. Ever.

If you have decided to live as one of the new poor, however, then the idea of getting a *home*, something sculpted around your life for you to live in, becomes almost an art form. And doing so without money, or with very little, makes it such a challenge that you soon realize, as we did, that it will take everything you've got and then some.

First, examine your life, as you want it from then on, and try to see if you can pin down some of your future needs. Do you want to live in a city, in the country? Getting a home in the city is much more difficult, as is living, but there are advantages—cultural things, libraries, theaters, etc.—to city living. In the country it is much easier to get a home, much easier to live, but there is no entertainment—no clutter, nothing to hold anything in as one friend visiting us said, his eyes almost moving out of his head. (He was from Milwaukee and he was looking across a thirty-mile expanse of wilderness.)

Decide which you want, then decide to some

A SURVIVAL GUIDE

extent how you want to live as well. With modern conveniences, rugged, primitive—they are all suitable ways to live, but your kind of home will depend on which you want.

Finally, your particular needs. Do you have children? Relatives living with you? (Heaven help you.) Pets? (A word on that, pets: They are a two-edged sword. They offer companionship and joy, but you have to feed them. There will be a cheap pet food recipe later in the food section; still, pets demand a little of what you do, so it's sometimes best to be rid of them if you can. We couldn't. In fact, we now have fourteen dogs, but they are sled dogs and our only form of transportation other than canoe so they aren't really pets. Sort of.)

Sit down and make another list, showing all that you think you'll need and all that you think your new poor-home will have to supply in the way and type of living area and then think about it for a few days. Don't jump into anything. In two or three days hit the list again and re-evaluate.

Downgrade everything into simplicity. If you have put four bedrooms do you *really* need four or would a hide-a-bed in the living room serve for one? Do you really *need* a quarter-acre playroom in the basement? A stable? A five-car garage?

Cut it all down as much as possible and then go into your needs from a purely realistic viewpoint. What does your new home really have to supply as far as your life is concerned? Do you just need shelter or do you need a more complete concept of the home—an environment? Also, do you wish to change to make a new kind of home or do you wish to bend the idea of home to fit the way you want to live? All these things matter a bit at the first, but they matter a lot more later.

If, for instance, you are living in a city or suburban environment, do you wish to change? The reason this might be important is that living in the city, and living poor, can be a bit more difficult than living in the country. In the country it is possible to turn the work of your back directly into food, heat, shelter; in the city it's necessary to earn money to pay for those things. And while it can be greatly curtailed, it is still necessary to have some and as anybody who is poor knows, sometimes it can be hard to get some money—especially when you really need the stuff. Like when the heating bill is due and it's cold and they're going to pull the plug, right?

If you're going to live in the city, a lot of the methods already mentioned will also provide a home. Look for run-down or abandoned places, caretaker jobs, etc. There are surprising numbers of them and while it may take time, usually in the end it will pay off; you will wind up with some form of shelter you can start with.

And that's all it is, a start. It is still not a home. It is necessary to shape it, change it to fit

A SURVIVAL GUIDE

your needs. Don't be afraid of this work, it isn't hard; remodeling might be a bit time-consuming, but it's easy to do if you have two hands and eyes. There are many good books on the subject; get them out of the library and study as you go. Remember not to be dismayed by the way your new home might look at the start. A little work will literally do wonders and all the the materials you need—paint, lumber, nails, etc.—can be picked up at yard and rummage sales, fire sales, that sort of thing. Open up and you'll find all sorts of stuff coming in.

The main thing about the remodeling is to take your time. If you put a time limit on anything it means spending money; if you take it slow and easy and work only as you can scrounge materials, it will almost all come in free. Look for buildings that are being torn down and get lumber, plumbing items, electrical things, whatever you need. (We know one person who built an entire home—two bedrooms, with a one-car garage standing separately—from a hotel they were tearing down in Colorado Springs, Colorado.) Just pile the items up where you are remodeling and use it as you go, working only as you get material. It means, obviously, that you are going to be living for some time in a place that's undergoing construction, but that's not as bad as it sounds if you seal off and do one room at a time or one area of the house at a time.

In the city the act of remodeling a house or

BEAT THE SYSTEM

run-down apartment into a home isn't nearly as hard as finding one in the first place—or finding one that doesn't take a fortune to pick up. And to a certain extent you are hammered into a money corner on this one—not a good place to be, but acceptable in a sense if you must continue to live in an urban area. In that case, if you must find a place involving money, then obviously the best thing to do is minimize the amount of money involved.

Try to work a deal with the seller-landlord, whatever. If it's somebody selling, get him down. No matter what they start at, work it down—think in terms of no money at all while you're talking to him about whatever the place is. Then, when it's low, or as low as you can get it, stretch things out to get the payments lower. In all cases, when you are poor, it is far easier to get small amounts of money than it is larger amounts—even if they have to be paid over a longer period of time, even if the interest paid is slightly higher.

Also make every attempt to turn your own personal work directly into some product you need. If you are buying a house that is run-down and badly in need of work, check to see if the person you are buying it from has any other such homes. It's likely they do, especially if they're in real estate. Trade your work on his other place for payments against the place you're buying—always work for product. Money is merely a storage device, and a very inefficient one at that. It's always best to use your work for direct things you can use. You can't eat or build with money, only with the things money can buy. So why work for the money when you can work directly for such things?

Two last thoughts about urban living. First, when you get into the home concept, try to get some land with it. Not a lot, but a decent-sized small piece for a garden (30 feet by 100 feet will do it). This will take on significant impact when you realize that on a piece like that you can grow almost all the food a family of three or four needs for an entire year at a cost of about thirty to forty dollars (at the time of this writing). It can be a tremendous aid and will be covered in the food section later.

Second, there are "hidden" government funds all over the place. Money for remodeling homes, money for fixing up neighborhoods, money for plumbing improvement, money for this and money for that—you'd have to be a computer to keep up with it all. But if you're living in a run-down area (likely), check with the state and federal agencies and see if there is any way you qualify for grants or low interest loans to help you fix your place up. It's very likely that you do and while the government hassle can be a pain—*will* be a pain—it may well be worth the effort. If you make a run on the government funding, make a complete run. Get anything and everything you can get in the way of housing funding; ask them if there's anything they know that you don't, any hidden stuff; they'll be glad to help. The more they help you the more they justify their jobs.

The keyword is flexibility when speaking about getting a home in an urban situation. Figure out your needs, your wants, then be ready to bend them slightly to fit the available opportunities. While it's true that in the country you can be slightly more particular, in the city there are so many regulations, so many demands, that it's difficult to get exactly what you want, at least at the start. You can perhaps come close and then remodel to suit your needs as you go along, but at first, stay wide open. Check all of the methods suggested—abandoned homes, caretaker jobs, government funding—and any others you might be able to come up with as well.

It may very well be that you not only get what you want, or something you can shape into what you want, but you'll wind up with extra. While you're rumbling around you'll probably come across many housing opportunities that aren't quite right for you, but might work for somebody else. Keep them on a list (*another* list) for later use; they will work well for you when you enter or start a barter-network. (More on this vital area in a bit.) Many people are looking for housing and knowing where some is can give you something good with which to start bartering.

A final word: Don't be alarmed at things that seem in bad disrepair. It can look pretty awful and still be easy to fix. Easily. This is stated because most run-down urban housing seems to have been vandalized by something very close to complete mongol hordes with their ponies and plunder. It can look terrible. But with work—not necessarily money, but work—it can readily be brought back.

Country living is a whole different ball of wax. Speaking now in terms of any rural situation, or wilderness, or in-between—or even in very minimally functioning or abandoned towns—it's all much the same as far as finding a home is concerned.

For one thing, one very important thing—in the country they have always been poor. Not as poor as other countries, perhaps, but they have always worked without money. It might be that working close to the land makes the nonsense of money diminish (we have found some of that), or it might be that the cities have just always needed more of everything and hence expanded into money. Whatever the reason, if you are poor in the country it is not only acceptable, in a way it's desirable.

If you go into the country with a lot of money, and spend it on things without working hard for those same things, you are in some ways received with some hesitation; not distrust, exactly, but not completely acceptance, either. If, however, you come poor and work for your

BEAT THE SYSTEM

food and shelter you are taken in and helped and made to feel welcome—as long as you work.

Finding a home in the country is largely a matter of choice rather than a matter of taking what you can get. Over the past seven or eight decades people have been migrating from the farms and country back to the cities—the pull of easy money being what it is. Some of them are moving back, but not many. So if you are willing to work there is much still available either very, very cheap or simply for the caretaking or to buy for back taxes or to trade for work.

The first choice is to decide where you want to live—which to some extent also means how. Moving into the country means living with the land and the land dictates method.

If you head for the southwest, as many do, remember that because of the energy crunch a lot of people have moved to warmer southern climates. *Crowded* is synonymous with *costly*. You can still live there being poor, but it is much harder and the land, arid, sometimes burnt, and desert, is much harder to live with. Water is more difficult to get, crops need more work to maintain. It can be done, and many who have done it swear that it's the best, and much better than living within the system. But it is demanding and you should take that into account.

Finding a house in the country is also a matter of choices. It is necessary to decide to some extent *how* you want live as well as where. There are some people who cannot farm, cannot make the ground work. And while they should still work a large garden (there will be a section later on power gardening in which *anybody* can make it work), those people have to consider other forms of work—not just for income in money, but in bartering materials.

One of the key concepts in this is cottage industry. Almost any of them can be done in any kind of home, but there are a few that demand specialization. If, for instance, you want to sell firewood then obviously your new home will have to be in a firewood-cutting area. That sort of consideration is elemental, but maybe something you should think about before you make the move. (For those who are in doubt there will be a list of potential cottage industries later in the book, compiled with their needs.)

Getting a home *out* of an urban environment comes down to being a matter of choice, more than anything else. First, you should know that under certain circumstances, for those who are dedicated and healthy and who have time (don't we all when we are poor?), there is a way to build a home, a good home, for virtually nothing. An entire house for, say, four hundred dollars. It will be covered shortly, but if you are going to commit to such an extreme venture— and you should also know that it takes one hell of a lot of work—you do not look for a home, per se. So the next little part may not apply to you.

BEAT THE SYSTEM

For those who are looking for something already constructed: one more choice. Do you want to just live for a time or do you want to own? If you're just looking for a place to settle for a long period, a few years, say, then many of the same rules as renting in the city apply—except that there are more places available (admittedly over a much wider area) and they will be decidedly cheaper.

To rent-live, look for abandoned farms, cottages, and the like. Get an old clunker car or some bicycles and cover some country. Don't be afraid to get in there and talk to people—farmers, people in the neighborhood. Tell them that you're looking for a place, explain that it has to be cheap, that you are willing to trade for work—don't be aloof. When you became poor, if you were like us, you lost a lot of the drive that causes snobbery. Or perhaps it's just that our snobbishness now takes on a different bent; I can now, for instance, sneer openly at any poor devil foolish enough to buy a Mercedes. Be as candid as you can, and honest, and you'll find many people opening up to you.

Examples of homes for temporary living came to us during research like a cloud. When we began looking, and asking, we were stunned to find how many people are living the way we are: Everyone from two girls living in an abandoned trapper's cabin in Alaska to a couple minding a resort in northern Michigan. Incidentally, the girls were trapping—they ran a hundred mile line with dogs—and the people at the resort helped run the place through the short summer months for a place to live all winter, with utilities included. Both examples show excellent use of capabilities and opportunities.

Other examples showed the same. One family moved into a secondary farm, run-down and going to ruin, bought out by a larger farmer. Their "rent" is to help during the peak load times, harvesting, planting, etc. For this work (about two and a half months a year) they received a place to live—a *good* place to live—all their heat and lights, all their meat and produce (which they have learned to process themselves), and a much more healthy environment than they had in the city.

While not true country living, one couple with a baby told us they were living in an old hotel in a very small town in North Dakota. The entire population of the town was sixty-three. But it had once boomed and the out-of-state owners of the old hotel didn't want the place to just go to ruin. They were happy to have someone live in it and keep it up—so happy they pay all utilities and for any materials needed in repair.

A single man who had been a systems analyst with a large firm in Los Angeles now lives on an island in a lake in northern Minnesota. The island is owned by a wealthy doctor in New York—one of those doctors who take out things that maybe don't need to be taken out and who make unbelievable amounts of money. He got sick of having boaters tear the place apart when he wasn't there. So when our subject approached him the doctor was more than glad to have him move in, after a suitable investigative process. During the two weeks that the doctor comes to fish for walleyes the analyst camps in a tent (*with* mosquito screening) at the other end of the island. The rest of the time he has the run of the island and a large home, with boats, canoes, all utilities paid.

There is a feeling, totally understandable, that these are rare occurrences. Often, when we first decided to make the jump the primary thought that entered our mind was: "Yes, they can do it, but can we? That's one isolated incident, but can many people do it—can *we* do it?"

What struck us, after we made the move and began our research, were the numbers of people who had become fed up and were doing the same. We met one couple who had been working at a bank in Iowa—the same bank. They got married and quit and went to a church camp in Wisconsin. This camp is on a small lake and is used for summer retreats, and for underprivileged kids in the summer. In the winter it's a white tomb; the pipes usually freeze and the place falls apart. This couple got the classic job of caretaking the camp. They get free room and free food (there is a large mess hall with attendant food supplies), *plus* about four grand a year for working to keep the place up. They have a small separate house of their own, boats available, tools—everything they need to live except clothing money. They even get to use the company or camp truck to go to town and don't have to buy gas for it.

While they are obviously something of an exception, the above couple shows wonderfully what can be done by spending a little extra time and effort looking for the right kind of thing.

Opportunity for homes is everywhere if you're going to live in the country. Just don't limit yourself and don't be discouraged. It might look a little weird at first, and be seemingly disappointing, but keep looking. Something good will come. It always does.

Building A Home For Absolutely Nothing. Almost.

Two assumptions first: one, that you have slightly more than average hand-eye coordination. Not great, but usable—can you use hand tools without losing various parts of your body? That kind of coordination. And two, that you can find some relatively inexpensive land somewhere on which you want to live (actually not that hard). Also, this land has to be outside the standard building code areas because if you play the game by the code strictly, it amounts to an added horrendous expense.

Those assumptions out of the way, there are a few more points to consider. The most important part to keep in mind is that time and money are parts of the same equation when it comes to living and building. If you have more money you can take less time to do something. On the other hand, if you have more time, you can take less money. It's that simple.

And if you have lots and lots of time, you almost don't need any money. This applies not just to building, but to all aspects of living poor. Now and then, just as a test, we use nothing from the outside world for a week—nothing— and manufacture everything for ourselves. It takes much time, but that's all it takes, and it's time that we aren't using to punch a clock in some miserable factory somewhere anyway, time that we now have for living. So it doesn't matter how much we use.

You must live hard and tight if you're going to build a home for nothing. Hard and tight the way Hemingway talks in *A Moveable Feast*, but not at the hard level of *The Good Earth*.

Get an older small trailer, if you can stand them, or one of those large tents. You can find them sometimes for nothing or next to nothing at surplus sales or backyard sales, and spend some of the first time setting up a camp on your land. Make this as livable as you can because you may be living in this way for some time. Dig a good privy (Isn't that a marvelous word? Privy?), one that's sanitary and well-covered and screened. And if you're truly going to rough it, make a good wood cooking area with rocks.

A SURVIVAL GUIDE

Not just a ring, but a barbeque shelf kind of arrangement so you can work on it as a stove. (These things have nothing to do with the home, but much to do with your comfort, which will make the home easier to do.) Camping, living rough, can be very easy if you take the time to make things correct when you do them. If you don't take the time it can all turn to garbage in minutes.

When you have a suitable rough home situation—mini-home, home-before-a-home—then look to the land. If you are in the southwest there is a good chance you can build with adobe or rock and mortar, using the materials available. These are both completely acceptable forms of housing—actually much better than movern materials—and relatively easy to do. "Relatively" because both are heavy materials and require some strength, but then all of building seems to require some strength. So in a way it's all the same—strength or ability to use levers and pulleys.

If you are in the central north, northwest or northeast, there is a chance you can use logs, also a very suitable form of building. In the south there is also cheap wood available.

In this form of free home building the most important thing is to let the land, the specific land you're building on and the terrain around, dictate what you will do. Use what nature provides—it is the oldest concept in building, and one that we have foolishly moved away from the most. In a very real way it is the only sensible way to build.

When you see the availability of material, whatever it is, go to the nearest library and get the appropriate building books. There are many on each form and most of them are adequate; some are very good. Rammed earth, adobe, rock, logs, rough-hewn wood, sod—there are books on all of them, books that will show you exactly what to do, step by step.

Don't start before you do the research, however, in that there is much added work and maybe a little madness. The people who wrote those books for the most part actually did the work involved and aside from a strictly how-to standpoint they can show you dozens of shortcuts that will save time and work. Read the book before you start slopping mud and straw into shoeboxes for bricks.

It is possible that in the end you might find just the right piece of land at just the right low price and not be able to find a local suitable form of building material. Although this would be very rare, it could happen: there could just be nothing about the land that lends itself to building a home.

In that case go ahead and set up the base camp arrangement, taking care to make it more settled than you might have in other situations. Make the latrine a little deeper, the cooking area a bit more elaborate.

Then go to the nearest settled town, the big-

A SURVIVAL GUIDE

ger the better, and start scrounging materials. Look for large old buildings that are being torn down, again the bigger the better—or better yet, buildings that are about to be torn down. There is constantly something being torn down and something new being put up in the cities—it's just a matter of finding the right something.

When you do, start bringing boards, windows, doors, all building lumber, old plumbing, wiring fixtures (not the wire itself) back to your home site. Get it all and then some, everything that's loose, and on those rare days when you can't scrounge stay home and clean up what you've brought back, pulling nails and such. It is miserable, filthy, grubby work, but in the end it can get you a home. A nice home. Used lumber, dried lumber, is better than new because it won't shrink.

Of course you will have to buy some few things—specifically, roll-roofing (it's the cheapest); insulation (unless you can recover some, not likely in truly old buildings); and wire (old wire tends to be a bit dicey to use). But it is genuinely amazing how much can be scrounged. Several people we know have built entire homes in this way and while it takes some time, in the end it's well worth it. Consider that if you go through the system you now spend close to a quarter of a million dollars on a house over a thirty-year period and if you go this way you might spend five hundred at the outside. The true economics of it come home with impact.

BEAT THE SYSTEM

This all sounds very hard, I know, and much of it is. I once tore apart an old hotel for the lumber and couldn't believe how dirty and hard it was; at one point I was almost crying in frustration and exhaustion. But it can be done. While it is physically demanding there is no great intellectual demand—just start pulling boards off with a crowbar and a large framing hammer, wearing goggles and a hardhat and heavy work gloves. It can be done and it isn't beyond doing for a free home, or virtually free home, if you are going to live poor.

As for amounts of lumber needed, it's pretty simple. A large old home with a garage will yield enough for a smaller new one without a garage. If you want to do the whole shot and have a garage plus a home, you might have to scrounge two older places.

Just keep telling yourself while you do it—it can be done.

A final thought. If you know nothing about building, as we did when we started all this, then there are several ways to learn. First and foremost, make a run on the library. As already discussed there are tons of books on the subject and they are all free and all helpful. Don't be afraid to teach yourself new areas of life.

But perhaps more important, watch the house you're tearing down as you work. Note how it was constructed—you can learn as much or more that way and get a feel for building while you're doing it.

A SURVIVAL GUIDE

A home can, quite literally, be anything. Primitive tribes in the southwest lived sometimes in small little brush hovels covered with skins and in the same area at the same time other tribes lived in complex mansions of stone and adobe that still stand after many hundreds of years. Both ends of the home spectrum were represented and both forms of home suited the individuals involved—the Apaches and the Pueblos.

Remember, in this whole idea of housing and a home, you're trying to find something that suits the way you want to live. So do it for yourself, not for some mythical architectural idea of what homes should be like. Take your time and do it the way you want it done.

Being poor can be an opportunity to improve the way you live, if you use it right.

5

GETTING FOOD

"In the great scheme of things it is necessary to eat. But where is it written that we *must* buy the food from the supermarket?"

Food.

With shelter out of the way, or in the process of being out of the way, the second thing to concentrate on is food. And in no other area of being poor is there as much potential confusion as there is surrounding the aspect of what one should put in one's mouth to sustain life.

At one time, and not too long ago at that, a person grew virtually all of his own food, be it vegetables or meat, or he hunted it. When he came to a product that he couldn't grow—salt, coffee, whatever—he either traded or bought it. But far and away most of the family food was grown by the family. In fact, this was common less than a hundred years ago—two lifetimes.

Now it is practically all "store-bought" and

the quality of that food has eroded to the point where eating some of it is not only not particularly nutritive, it is downright unhealthy and sometimes (over the long haul) potentially fatal.

Our own situation was probably typical. At the peak of our upper middle class career, or lower upper class, or whatever, we ate-lived some pretty strange habits. We spent over eight hundred dollars a month on food, or on materials from the store—some of them would defy being termed food, although we ate them. Much of this monthly intake consisted of fast-foods, convenience foods—dried potatoes; frozen precooked things like chicken and French fries. And I realize now (though at the time I couldn't see it) that the only reason we bought the fast-foods was so we wouldn't spend the time cooking that we could use to go out and earn more money to buy more fast-foods, so we could save more time to earn more money to get more convenience foods . . . and so on.

Eight hundred a month. Actually about eight forty, average, and for this we gained weight and lost health at a truly astounding rate. It is true that many people are sensible about eating—although you probably can't be sensible and still buy mass-produced food—but we weren't. We enjoyed it too much, we really did. We liked to get some steaks and potatoes and gravy—all premixed and prefrozen—and sit down to a good heavy meal. It was the way we lived.

It was wrong, at least for us. But more than

being wrong, it soon destroyed itself, as do all forms of overindulgence. Even had we not lost money and lost the ability to buy all the convenience foods, all the rich foods, the style of eating would soon have destroyed us—signs of approaching cardiac problems were there already and it would have been a very short time until health would have eliminated us.

As it was our financial downfall saved us. And simply because it was forced on us doesn't detract from the significance of the salvation.

We spent just over eight hundred a month on food, as I said, and we now spend—total—just over forty. That's forty dollars a month, on all forms of "store-bought" stuff. The methodology of that shift is worth studying, especially when you take into account that we eat much better now than we ever have and that we have a far greater diversity of food now than we had back in those good old fat days.

When we became poor we suddenly noticed that there were many foods we could no longer afford. It was as simple as that, but the concept was so profound that it shook us into viewing, or reviewing, our relationship with the food we ate.

To be unable to get certain food because we could no longer afford it meant that some outside force could control something as vital to our life as food—some force other than God or weather. It probably sounds pretty simple to most, but for us it was an unsettling thing to realize, the final indication of the invasion of our lives that had occurred with seeming opulence, or affluence.

We were appallingly ignorant. When it came right down to it our whole concept of getting food meant going to the store. And the longest time we had ever thought about getting food ahead was on the order of ten days.

Then I read an article in one of those gardening magazines that said an eastern state—I think it was Massachusetts—would starve in three weeks if the trucks quit bringing the food supplies in. There just isn't enough food grown in that state long enough ahead to feed the population.

So our first step, we thought, was clear. We had to learn. We had to find a way to learn to grow and raise our own food, something we had damn near forgotten genetically. But in the meantime, while we learned we still had to eat. And so acquiring good food, cheaply, without knowing how to grow it, became our true first step.

It took us a time to realize it, or to believe it, but there is a basic truth about grocery stores that shook us to our cores: They don't manufacture food. They are, truly, unnecessary. All the typical grocery store does is to take in prepack-

A SURVIVAL GUIDE

aged grocery items and sometimes slightly raw materials (corn that needs to be washed, etc.), and put them on a shelf for us to come in and buy. They don't generate any of the food, grow it, or even process 90 percent of it—they just take it in, put it on a shelf, and sell it to you.

For a whopping profit.

There's the crux of the matter—that whoping profit. We pay them millions and millions of dollars just for putting something on a shelf so we can reach up and take it down and put it in a cart and give them money for it.

That hit us like a stampede. We were paying a lot of money and if we wanted to save all that money all we had to do was skip the stores. If they didn't grow the food, or raise it, or produce it, all we had to do was find where it was grown and raised and produced and buy it direct and save all that money we had been spending.

And that was exactly what we did and it is the primary step for everyone to take when living poor and still eating relatively well.

If at all possible go directly to the farmer. Those potatoes come out of the ground, and a farmer grows them and usually gets only a very small percentage of what the store charges you. If you go to the farmer and offer him half of what the store charges you—only half—he will still be making probably three or four times what he normally makes on the product.

Even if you live in the middle of the city, try

BEAT THE SYSTEM

to get out to the surrounding farms and buy direct from the source because what happens between that source and the point you get it at the supermarket is, in my opinion, so bad it amounts to something very close to rape.

Consider wheat. It's basic, makes our bread—the staff of life. At the time of this writing the farmer gets about three dollars a bushel for wheat. A bushel weighs sixty pounds. If you buy that wheat in the form of bread, in the store, you will be paying something on the order of *fifty-five* dollars for the same bushel of wheat. The manufacturer grinds it up (you can get hand grinders for just over forty dollars), makes it into loaves, and bakes it (bread is easy to make), while the store marks up the price over fifteen times for their minimal effort. You can buy the same wheat direct from the farmer, wash it in water, grind it (whole wheat is more healthy anyway), and make a much better loaf of bread for a tiny bit over a nickel than you can buy. If I buy a loaf of bread right now it costs ninety cents and there's very little food value in it. If I make it, it costs a nickel and it will provide food.

And that is the normal concept of the store, that kind of profit edge is what they try to get on everything.

So go to the farmer. Check around the city you live in and see what crops are grown and buy in bulk form direct. Pay more than the farmer would have gotten at market prices, if

A SURVIVAL GUIDE

you wish, and you'll still save hundreds and hundreds of percent.

You might find a truck farm with many different kinds of vegetables. There are many farmers turning to this versatile form of farming as the energy crunch makes it unprofitable to use fuel for moving vegetables long distances. Truck farms will cost a bit more than standard bulk farmers, but they will still be far below the stores and usually—almost always—the product you get will taste better and not have suffered so much from handling.

The same goes for meat. Those animals are grown on farms and ranches and they'll sell you meat in bulk form. Get a good book on cutting meat up (there are many; even the government has a few good ones), a meat saw, a few good knives, and do your own.

I know how that sounds, and the first time we looked at a half a small pig on the kitchen table I felt the same way. My gosh, I thought, is there a pork chop in *that?* But there was, and after some initial fumbling we found it and many others and are now quite adept at carving meat. And all the fat we carve off and don't eat we save for pet food, a kind of double benefit. It was hard at first, or a little bit scary, but it's surprisingly easy to do a passable job and save yourself tons of money. (Of course, now we also grow all our own meat and food so we've taken it still further. But more of that later.)

BEAT THE SYSTEM

If you live in an area where there just aren't any farms around—some parts of the desert, perhaps in truly large cities—you can still save a substantial amount of money by buying in bulk. Look for warehouse situations, or people who sell produce directly out of trucks, that sort of thing, and then buy enough to last for a time (a few months). You can build a small storage box or corner in a room with a few boards and keep potatoes or other semiperishables for a surprisingly long time without spoilage.

Finally, if you must buy food and there aren't any farms around and you can't seem to find anything in bulk, check farmers' markets and the like first. Then remember the maxim of the poor: Look for the deal.

The one thing that struck me perhaps most about living without much money is the often major difference in prices between very similar stores. Of course the food stores have all their tricks, like loss leaders and other things to suck you in, and you should look for those deals as well. But there is quite often a truly striking difference in the same brand just by going to two different stores. We sometimes saw up to 30 and 40 percent difference in prices in stores eight blocks apart, and 10 percent is common.

So dig and look for the best price on food as well as everything else you have to buy.

A SURVIVAL GUIDE
Places Where Food Is Cheaper:

Day-old bakeries.

Warehouse food supplies—where you buy it by the case and carry it out yourself, etc.

Damaged goods stores—where they sell dented cans, caved-in boxes of food.

Restaurant suppliers—often they'll have extra food and no way to move it through their normal buyers. Not always productive, but very much worth a check.

Any major institutional supplier who might have large amounts of food from odds and ends of orders.

"Dated" material from regular stores. They are not supposed to sell it for food, but check (tell them it's for pets) and use your own judgment as to whether it's really dated or not. We once got sixty-five pounds of whipping cream that a store had overordered and had gone past date on. While we couldn't use it as cream, we did take a mixer and make almost thirty pounds of butter. It was delicious, too. Dated, dried bread can be reconstituted by steaming for a few minutes—you'll swear it was fresh-baked.

The ultimate step in this business of removing obstacles between you and the source of the food is obviously to grow it yourself and remove all the middlemen. And what you can save, if you make a large enough garden and work at it hard enough, is very eye-opening.

Growing your own food, whether it be a garden or a large farm, is probably the most elemental act the human can perform, along with hunting. It is so basic, so nearly primitive, that the majority of people seem to have forgotten how to do it. I fell into that category. I knew you turned soil, that you planted the seed, and that was about it.

I didn't know how to plant, when to plant, what to plant, or how much to plant. Assuming I could have gotten something into the ground and have gotten it likewise to come up, I didn't know how to tend it, how to judge what it would do, or how to harvest and keep it through the winter and summer until the next garden would come in to feed me.

In two years—two short years—I have progressed from that state of agricultural ignorance to growing virtually all my own food. The process of that progression, of that move, something that started nearly imperceptibly and moved with lightning speed, is worth cataloging.

We found some books at the library, books on gardening and soil, and sat down in the three months of northern winter before the snow went—three months after we moved into an old trailer—and started to study about gardening.

The first thing that hit us is that if we did it my way—my wife was more astute in this matter than I was—and just put the seed in the ground

A SURVIVAL GUIDE

and waited, we would in all probability starve to death.

There was more to it than that. On the other hand, I couldn't believe some of the technical jargon either. There were government-oriented pamphlets that nearly had us going into calculus to figure out our soil content and the planting procedures. I didn't think it could possibly be that complicated.

The answer, as in all things, lay somewhere between the two extremes. We couldn't just throw the seeds out the window and hope for a crop, but on the other side we didn't have to get a doctorate in applied agricultural techniques either.

All we had to do was work. Hard.

We rented a tiller and thoroughly chewed up an area thirty by one hundred feet the first year—one of the books had said three thousand square feet would feed a family for a year. It won't, but we tried that first year.

Next, we went back to the book and learned what kinds of vegetables to plant where—yes, it matters what's next to what. Since we were in the north we had to go to a greenhouse and buy partially grown tomatoes, squash, cabbage, and peppers. (The second year we started our own in a kitchen window and saved the money.)

We were two weeks getting it all in, but when we were done we had tomatoes, cabbages, kolrabi, turnips, carrots, potatoes, corn, five different squashes, lettuce, radishes—everything. There were many more, all planted in neat rows.

Then we sat back and waited for it all to come in and feed us. That was the impression we got from all the gardening books we'd read. If careful attention were paid to planting and tilling the soil you could expect a good crop. We did not know about Peterson's Primary Law of Gardening, which states, simply put, that all weeds grow faster than any edible plants by a factor of ten.

In ten days the garden looked like a jungle, just a mass of things coming up. And we were happy until we discovered that none of it was coming in neat rows, but all over the place.

We went back to the books and found the part we'd missed about weeds, the part that says you have to get down there on your hands and knees and pick them out with your claws or they will take over the entire world, starting with your garden.

In fact, that first year we missed a lot. The weeds almost won before we got to work on them, and then we didn't get a good yield because our soil was too acid (cured with hardwood ashes sprinkled liberally everywhere), and we still wouldn't have gotten a good yield because there was too much sand and it was too dry that year and the soil-sand wasn't all that rich.

But we fed ourselves for six and a half months on that initial feeble attempt. Six months without having to go to the store except for condi-

A SURVIVAL GUIDE

ments and margarine and flour and hamburger. We fed ourselves with higher quality for that six months; with food that tasted better and was better for us than the "store-bought" kind. We fed ourselves handsomely for those six months but more, much more, we found that we *could* feed ourselves—something we'd thought impossible because we'd been locked into the stores for too long—and we found the true secret of gardening, at least for us.

Plant big, more than you think you'll need. Any extra can be sold or bartered off easily. But most important, be ready to work for what you get: In gardening, perhaps more than anything else, the amount of work you put in is directly porportional to the amount of food you get out. The second year we doubled the size of the garden, went to a neighbor who raised horses and brought in twenty-two pickup loads of manure for fertilizer, put hardwood ashes everywhere (we'd been heating with birch so that worked out well—while we're on it, coal ashes don't work), then hoed or plucked every weed as fast as they came to the surface.

Our yield was wonderful. Over the last year we increased by four. There were vegetables everywhere—it seemed the house was full. We not only fed ourselves for the entire year but had massive amounts left over to give friends, to barter for meat and milk at a nearby farm and, finally, to help feed another neighbor's pig for which we got a front quarter.

BEAT THE SYSTEM

We are now, obviously, hooked on growing our own and feel cheated when we have to buy something at the store, even salt or pepper.

A word of caution: it is the purpose of this book to show how in general terms it is possible to garden successfully. And we have done it for ourselves. But it would be impossible to explain everything that needs to be known for all things pertaining to gardening in the narrow confines of a single chapter. For that reason we earnestly recommend going to the library and getting as many books as you can on gardening before you start.

For those who cannot make the commitment to a gigantic garden in hopes of harvesting enough food for the year, you can of course stop anywhere along the way—plant whatever you want or think you'll need.

But there are two approaches to consider before going to it. First, as most people do, you can plant a small amount of a lot of things—what they used to call a kitchen garden in the old days, and I guess still do. Something for salads and soups and quick snacks while it's coming in—and such a garden can be beneficial. The produce is better than you can get at the store and tastes wonderful. Kitchen garden specialties can also cut down some of the cost of groceries. If you spend a lot of money on potatoes, for instance, then put the entire small

A SURVIVAL GUIDE

garden in spuds and see if you can get enough for the year. Since in a way it's easier to grow a lot of one thing than it is smaller amounts of lots of things—less complicated—specialized gardening could be said to be more efficient. Still, it doesn't give the variety that's so nice in the late summer when the gardens begin to come in. It's very much a matter of personal judgment.

For some reason many people who garden seem to become vegetarians. We didn't keep an exact percentage, but a surprising number of the people we interviewed for this book had gone from eating meat to dropping it when they got into gardening.

We didn't.

Unfortunately, just because we decided to remain carnivores the meat prices didn't go down. They hung up there between frightening and outrageous. As a matter of fact, they are getting worse all the time.

It became rapidly clear that if we were going to continue as meat eaters we were either going to have to find a cheaper source, hunt, or raise our own. Or all of the above.

We chose all of the above and the methods we found are listed below.

BEAT THE SYSTEM
Cheaper Sources of Meat:

As with vegetables, we started searching out neighboring farms. It was harder than finding vegetables, but we finally did locate sources for pork and beef that were direct.

The difficult part about getting meat directly from the farmer is that you'll probably have to kill it and cut it up yourself. We didn't know how at first and the first time we killed a hundred pound pig (actually too small to slaughter, but we didn't know about meat efficiency then) it was like watching a really bad Scandinavian art film from the mid-Sixties.

We had a book, of course, that showed how to slaughter and dress (gut) and cut up, but that's all we had. We rapidly found there is a difference between a drawing of where to cut away a pork chop and an animal running around on the ground. Suffice to say we wound up with a lot of ground sausage (grinding the meat is a wonderful way to cover your mistakes) and a hearty respect for professional butchers.

It can however, be done. We are quite good at it now. The amount of money we save killing and cutting our own is astounding.

Two things to take note of if you intend buying large meat from the farmer and doing your own: You obviously need a place to do it, a large area that can get dirty, and you can't be squeamish. It is very messy work, and bloody, and there are unpleasant smells associated with the whole business of killing and death. (We can't eat meat for two or three days after killing and cutting because the smell lingers that long.)

A word of caution before proceeding: It is necessary to know fairly well what you are doing. And the worst time to find out, we found, is just after you kill the animal. There are no dotted lines on the things, no easily discernable places to cut this way or that. So get some books from the library and study them well before you slaughter and cut. It can make a fierce difference.

Smaller animals (chickens, rabbits, ducks, geese, etc.) are easier to handle, naturally, in all respects. And buying live to slaughter can save tremendous amounts of money. But there is a drawback in that fowl, specifically chickens, must be plucked and the feathers are a nuisance. Still very much worth doing, however.

It is recognized that most people will not be able to go to the farmer and buy live animals direct. There simply aren't enough farms close to cities.

It is, however, possible to buy meat in bulk form, already killed and dressed and cut into halves or quarters. Investigate this possibility by going to meat warehouses or large suppliers and see if you can buy partially processed meat. It will still be much cheaper than the stores and probably fresher.

The same holds true for small animals. Don't

ever buy cut-up chickens or rabbits if you can save by buying them whole. You might have trouble the first time or two when you cut, as we did, but after that the skill will come and in no time it becomes easy.

And look for deals on bulk meat. You might get a chance to pick up twenty or thirty chickens at a greatly reduced price. Always keep an ear to the ground for such things and try to have a little money or bartering material held back for lucky breaks.

It is all well and good to save money when you shop for things, but as a final message on procuring food it's important to remember that if you are truly poor—as we were and are—then even shortcuts can't handle it all.

To make it with little or nothing you will have to grow all your own food and meat (if you aren't a vegetarian), or grow a major part of it. Going to the stores is murder, no matter how you look at it, and the only way to stop that murder is to essentially furnish your own store. We found that anything less, any kind of compromise, quickly sucked us back into spending more and more in the market.

It is probably all scientifically done, but the way supermarkets seem to work on us can be particularly ruinous. All the pretty displays, all the fetching come-hither signs pull us in and

A SURVIVAL GUIDE

make us first salivate and then become openly hungry and then . . . buy.

And buy still more, until we are back in the same trap, spending money we don't have for food that we don't need and that isn't good for us anyway.

To really make it, try to grow all your own—or get into a bartering position with somebody who does grow it all.

Stay out of the stores.

6

BUILDING KNOWLEDGE AND GETTING BY

> "The main problem with money is that it's not genuinely *good* for anything. You can't even use it for grommet fodder. It's too small and too hard."

Bartering is, of course, an ancient form of trade. Economists tell us that it's a part of our economic system and that the primary reason it supposedly died out and was replaced by money is that it's too unwieldy. The classic example, I think, was the one told to me: "Take the case of the man who wants to own a ship and has the proper amount of coal to trade for it. He can't very well carry the coal to the man who owns the ship, can he? But if he turns the coal into money, then he can carry that and pay for the ship."

The scary part about that analogy is that our whole system is based on it and yet as far as I can tell—most certainly with us on a personal

BEAT THE SYSTEM

basis—hardly anybody wants to own a ship.

We want food.

And shelter.

And clothing.

And a lot of other things that are *easy* to carry. We have found that bartering, good old fashioned horse-trading, works very well and has saved us countless headaches, not the least of which is hassling with the banks. If you barter, we have found, you don't deal with checks and that has meant we haven't had to go into banks to try and cash said checks and put up with all the problems they hand out when they release your money to you. If for no other reason, bartering is worth it just to avoid the bank problem.

The nice thing about bartering is that establishing a bartering system, a network, is truly easy. What you're going to do, basically, is try to eliminate the need for money and if you keep it on that simple level, keep that in the back of your mind, it makes everything fall into place.

Try to barter for everything. Of course there are certain things where bartering might not be feasible—the power companies, for instance, or water or gasoline—but try it whenever you can. Any service (dental, health, car repair work) can be paid for with barter if you look around, and once you have dealt with somebody on a barter basis you can go back to that place again and again. It becomes part of your bartering network.

As for what you can trade, it might be anything. Don't limit yourself. Perhaps you have surplus vegetables, or you can do carpentry repair work, or painting, or cleaning—you can trade anything for anything. And when all else fails all you have to do is ask if there's anything they want or need, any product or service you might be able to furnish.

Then there's secondary bartering. Once you've got your network started keep a written record of what service or produce needs what. As the net expands you will find that you can trade on a three- and even four-way basis. You can work for one person who will do a service for another so that you can get something from the second one. It sounds as if it can get a bit complicated, and it can, but once it's going and you keep a written record of it all you'll find it simple to keep up. And the benefits are definitely worth it.

The problem with money, with dealing in money, is that since it has no worth of its own you must pay people to handle it for you. Banks take a cut, as do stores, etc.; all take a profit-cut, and all of that comes out of what you've worked to earn. It's just not good business.

If you clean somebody's front lawn and they in turn give you thirty pounds of potatoes, it's a straight-across arrangement with no profit cuts being taken out. You don't have to earn more than you need just to pay off the banks, etc., and in the final analysis you'll come out way ahead. In the long run inflation only affects money. If you're living by bartering, even only partially, and are swapping services, most of inflation's bullets will go over your head.

A note in conclusion: There is some talk as this is being written that the tax people are going to tax bartering, or that they feel tax should be paid on services or products bartered because it constitutes income. As the point of this writing, a rancher in Nebraska was having a bit of difficulty with the tax department—*They* were going to make him pay tax on working with his neighbors during roundup because they, in turn, would come back and work with him when he did *his* roundup and *They*, the tax people, said that the work they reimbursed him constituted income and that he, the rancher, would have to pay tax on it.

It is not the specific purpose of this book to point up the insanity of our economic system, although *somebody* ought to do such a book, but on this taxing of bartering thing you'll have to work it out yourself.

If you don't have any money then I don't suppose you can pay them in money and as for what percentage of service or pdoduct they will demand or how they will turn it into money or how they will arrive at what figures—I don't see how it can be anything but confusing. Just thinking about it makes parts of my brain numb.

Imagine being taxed on helping your neighbors. If you wrote that in a story or a book,

A SURVIVAL GUIDE

wrote that an economic system is taxing the help people give to one another, it wouldn't fly. Nobody would touch it. It boggles the mind.

Cottage industry.

There are some people, more and more every day, who claim that our system is breaking down, that there will be rioting in the streets and starvation and a whole raft of other disasters that certainly paint a bleak picture. And indeed, there are indications that such a breakdown may be coming; runaway inflation, mad laws, overburdening government.

But even if they're wrong, there is a booming business going on in cottage industries—which amounts to a breakdown and decentralization of the manufacture of goods. More people are building more things on their own and depending less and less on the outside world to provide them with goods.

It is an area ripe with opportunity because if you can establish a cottage industry of your own, it not only gives you a way to pick up a few dollars now and then to pay those bills that demand hard, cold, money, but also puts you in a better position to get solidly into a bartering network because you'll have a steady, consistent product going out that people will know about.

As to how to go about establishing a cottage industry, it's about as easy as falling over. Just

BEAT THE SYSTEM

pick something you like to do or manufacture and start doing it.

It can, quite literally, be anything. Following is a list of cottage industries that we found working very successfully when we did research:

Making picnic tables.
Making wooden lawn furniture.
Making sausage.
Weaving.
Pottery.
Making cheese.
Making wine.
Making knives.
Making muzzle-loading rifles.
Making indoor furniture.
Making cabinets.
Making toys.
Making pet food.
Making pet equipment.
Making equipment for horses (bridles, etc.).
Making rugs.
Making counter tops.
Making small kitchen utensils.
Making wood stoves.
Making work wagons.
Making hoes.
Making wooden easels.

There were many more, but the main point is that it can be almost anything. Watch for whatever opportunity presents itself, whatever people need or can use that you can provide; then go with the flow.

A SURVIVAL GUIDE

When we finally broke away and moved to the woods I ran a small trap line. It was good for a few dollars and brought in quite a lot of meat in the form of small game hunted while I was running the line (more on hunting later), and in a very real sense was a kind of cottage industry, since we live in something not unlike a cottage.

But as the line expanded the next year a friend introduced me to the use of sled dogs. I acquired a small team (six dogs) through bartering and found some old drawings of ancient Eskimo work sleds in an old book on the north. I made a work sled out of local birch, using the same methods described in the book, and used it on my line and for trips to town and the like for several months that winter.

Other people with dogs noticed the sled, asked about it, then ordered some for their own use. Before I really knew what was happening I was back-ordered several sleds and a new cottage industry was born—at least new for me.

One couple we talked to had decided to completely drop away from the system and carried it to the extent of going back in time to using old methods of building their house. Since old methods require old tools he wound up making all his own early American tools—wooden planes, shingle-splitting froes, etc.—to use as he built his home. Somebody came by, noticed the tools, asked if he could make more, and

BEAT THE SYSTEM

now they supply all their money needs by manufacturing pre-1800 tools.

Take advantage of whatever opportunity comes along—that's the true secret to a successful cottage industry. Don't make ceramic ashtrays with a picture of the Washington Monument on them when people want sleds for kids.

And the last thing, but equally as important: Keep it small. There is a tendency in all business to grow beyond sense. As the orders start coming in and more people want whatever product you are making, a kind of madness comes creeping in, a madness that demands that you grow and expand and plow more money back into the business and grow and expand still more, and still more until you are making lots and lots of money and working your ass off all the time, and either you develop a cardiac or get truly huge, call yourself Chrysler, and go under.

There's no sense to it. Keep it small so you can handle it and so you can enjoy your life rather than getting back into that terrible race that brought you down in the first place. In the end you are not being poor to turn it into being rich, or at least most people aren't. We are being poor to try and improve the quality of our life—a paradox that really works if you stay with it. Getting back into the insanity of the system will do just the opposite.

A SURVIVAL GUIDE

Hunting.

Moral issues aside on whether or not it's right to hunt and kill game for meat, there is a very practical side to it.

If you go into a store and try to buy meat, *any* meat, you get a very possibly substandard product at a very definitely outrageous price.

Chicken costs what good steak used to cost and if you eat meat, or would like to eat meat, the amount of money you spend or the bartering you must do is awful. In the woods there is cheap and very good lean meat for the taking if you spend a little time at it and if you live in an environment that allows hunting.

Hunting is not difficult. We are not talking now about the once-a-year hunters who go out and shoot each other trying to get a deer. That is not economical hunting. Most of those people who hunt deer once a year spend far more money than they ever get back in meat. On any kind of average based on logic, if you took the numbers of deer hunters versus the numbers of deer taken each year, and the amount of money spent, the venison probably comes out close to fifty dollars a pound.

But there is another kind of hunting, a kind that is enjoyable and legal and sporting and yet brings in meat on a consistent basis. Hunting small game and fishing are the two best ways to ensure a steady protein income—assuming, of course, that you live close to huntable land.

BEAT THE SYSTEM

For small game you need a suitable weapon and if you have not hunted much before it is a good bet to stay away from rifles. They demand some ability and they carry too far for safety considerations unless you know well what you are doing.

If you are a novice or a new hunter, about the best all-around weapon for small game hunting is a small, single shot shotgun—.410 gauge or .20 gauge. If you get larger you get into some recoil and you gain nothing in killing potential (unless you are going to hunt ducks and that's an art form unto itself). Those two shotguns will kill all small game in North America and are not uncomfortable to shoot.

Ammunition is another area where it's best to stay general. For all around work, probably the best size shot to buy is #6—it will take rabbits, all game birds (although for small birds, dove and quail, you will want smaller shot—therefore a larger number—to ensure better hitting), squirrels, and any of the so-called rough animals you might run into (raccoons, porcupines, etc.).

As for what to hunt—all meat is edible. That might sound a bit tasteless for those used to packaged, wrapped meat in the stores. But the truth is, if you have the stomach for it you can eat skunk, snake, lizard, anything, and it will be passable. We often eat porcupine, rabbit, raccoon, beaver, muskrat, as well as the more accepted forms of game—grouse, ducks, etc. One trapper we know eats fox—we haven't been able to because it stinks so awfully when you skin it—and swears that it's delicious meat.

So get a license and find out what you can hunt in your area and go hunting, after you get the necessary permission to use the land, if it's required in your area. All safety rules should be strenuously followed, of course, for your own safety as well as that of others and if you have any doubt about what you are shooting at, don't shoot. Period.

Some tips: Walk slowly, pausing often, and try to look back *into* brush and undergrowth. There is a tendency to let your eyes gloss over the surface of the brush and miss the game inside it. As you aim at the animal you are going to shoot, and assuming there is time, put the bead of the shutgun sight right on the head. That way it will be a quick kill, and also if it's close the shot load won't ruin the meat on the body. Don't worry about missing. If it's farther away the shot pattern will spread and still put enough shot in the body for a clean kill.

Care of game is simple. I carry rubber gloves—just some of those cheap ones from the market—and on rabbits I drop the entrails in the woods to check for tuleremia, a disease of rabbits that can be passed to humans. Wearing the gloves, open the body area and check the liver:

if it has white spots or cysts, leave the animal where it is—it is suspect. It still may not have the disease, but it's not worth messing with. Game birds don't have this problem and you can carry them home before cleaning if you wish.

Whether birds or rabbits or squirrels, the easiest method of cleaning is to skin. Plucking game birds is difficult and time-consuming and probably not worth the effort. Entrails, not counting stomach sections, can be kept and boiled with grains for pet food. (See the section on recipes.)

Cooking game is essentially the same as cooking domestic meat, except that it leans toward being tough, because game has to move a lot and move fast to stay alive. For this reason it is also usually very lean (ducks and beaver are the exceptions to this, and, of course, geese). So game works best in stews, or pressure-cooked a bit before roasting or frying. (More on this later in recipes.)

A word of warning about "hunting" in the city. There is much talk of Hemingway living for a time in Paris by nailing pigeons as they came down to feed. And pigeon is delicious meat. But that was back before chemicals were put into grains. Seed grains are treated to avoid various diseases or rot. Since pigeons get around considerably, and often feed on spilled grain in railroad yards, and since some of that grain may not be healthy, it is advisable not to eat city birds.

7

CARS

> "Life is like an onion. You keep peeling away the layers to get to the good part. But if you peel away too much, you don't have an onion."

Automobiles have become one of the true luxuries of modern life. What makes it difficult to accept and deal with is that for four or five decades they have ingrained themselves into our lives to the point where they became practically necessary for survival.

For many people who live in city areas, and especially if that area is a sprawling city like Los Angeles, it is for all practical purposes impossible to get along without some form of automotive transportation. A cheap store might be thirty or forty miles from your home and such distances make walking impractical—although in emergency situations it can be done.

The problem with cars and how they apply to living poor, obviously, is that they cost so much

BEAT THE SYSTEM

money to run and almost no part of running one of them can be bartered. You can't whip into your local Standard station with a bushel of tomatoes and swap them for gas—at least usually. It is, however, worth a try.

They want money for gas. And oil. A lot of money, considering what you get for it, and the only way to approach the concept of using an automobile—the only way if you truly *must* live where you need one—is to daily almost literally attack the expense.

Every chance you get, every single opportunity that comes along, don't start the engine, don't use the car. That's the primary thing to remember. If you run it you must spend money, if you don't run it you don't have to spend money. So leave the key off and every chance you get walk or ride a bike or use mass transit or don't take the trip. Evaluate every auto use, from long to the short, and fight to not run the car—that comes before any of the other money-saving guidelines and is far and away the most important. Apply that kind of thinking to all other parts of the automotive world as well. Stubbornly resist every expense.

Automobile insurance is probably one of the biggest expenses involved with driving a car and it's the first one to attack. Through one lobby and another the insurance companies have weaseled the concept of automobile insurance into the law in many states. It is illegal to operate a car without some stipulated minimum

A SURVIVAL GUIDE

amount of liability insurance. (One man we interviewed told us, concerning car insurance: "The truly remarkable basis of liability insurance as it applies to automobiles is the reverse logic of it—in truth, if you actually *need* liability insurance, they couldn't afford to sell it to you."

But even with insurance having the law working for it, you needn't simply accept the sting and live with it. You can look for the cheapest insurance, the very cheapest minimal amount you need to obey the law, and go with that. Shop around, really work at it, and try to get the one you pick to cut the price still more. Nothing is hard and fast. They are selling a service, just like any other business, and they are asking a fee—that doesn't mean you have to pay it. And when you consider that you will probably, mathematically, never get anything for the money you give them (they are betting on it), it makes the expense even more pointless. So fight it. Tear at this first expense until it is as low as possible and then let that be your guideline in all your further dealings with the car. Fight each expenditure as much as you can.

The true problem with automobiles is that you get almost nothing for the money you spend. For all the hundreds and hundreds—thousands—of dollars put into the things all you really wind up with is a minimal service: It is a machine to take you from one point to another, usually with a maximum of expense and maximum of waste and a maximum of stink and pollution. For this, you pump money into the tank and engine and that money never comes back, never truly gives you any kind of a product and is, simply, gone.

Look for the cheapest gas that will run the car; find the least expensive oil, run it well past the recommended changing time, and then save it in jugs for lubrication uses. And if you must do repair work do it yourself if you possibly can. There are many excellent books on individual cars at the libraries. Mechanical work—to the point where it takes special tools—is like anything else: If they can do it, you can do it.

Following are some of the easier things to do for yourself:

Change the tires (obviously).
Replace wiper blades (frustrating until you figure the little catch-out).
Replace fan belt.
Fix windows that don't roll up (just remove the door panel and it's simple).
Change the oil (get the manual for your car at the library).
Change spark plugs (you must buy a special little cheap wrench, but even then it's cheaper than a mechanic).
Change the points (again, get a manual on your car from the library).
Check and add antifreeze to the radiator (have the gas station attendant check it, then buy cheap at a discount and add it yourself).

A SURVIVAL GUIDE

Replace a faulty thermostat (get the manual, but it's easy).

Replace the air cleaner (it's that big drum thing over the carburetor on top of the engine).

Replace fuses (check if a light quits or some other electrical malfunction occurs—they are little glass and metal cylinders most often up under the dash on a little panel).

Replace burned-out lights (they sell numbered, coded lights at gas stations and usually all it takes is a screwdriver).

Replace floor mats, etc. (if you want to).

Check the oil (just pull the oil dipstick—usually a finger-ring-thing sticking up alongside the engine. Wipe it with a rag, put it back down firmly, pull it out again, and see where the oil is on the little lines on the stick. I realize that almost everybody knows how to do this already, but there were some we interviewed who didn't).

Check the transmission fluid (same kind of dipstick as the oil, only located sticking up out of the transmission).

There are quite a few secondary difficult jobs that can be done for yourself if you have the ability and knowledge, jobs that can save you a tremendous amount of money when it comes to repair. But they couldn't be classified as easy. You must know how.
They include:

Replacing brakes.
Checking and changing timing.

BEAT THE SYSTEM

Anything to do with air conditioners.
Replacing radiator hoses (actually not too bad, but a little demanding).
Replacing the battery (also not too hard except that it's heavy and messy).
Replacing generator or alternator.
Replacing voltage regulator.
Replacing heater.

A point to remember about the above jobs is that you'll need some special mechanic's tools—a good small socket set with an extension and maybe a small set of box- and open-end wrenches. But even if they cost a little more than you wanted to spend, they'll still be more than paid for on the first home repair job you do and well worth the expense.

There are, finally, some jobs you just about can't do for yourself unless you are a skilled mechanic—overhauls, rings, valves, replacing engines or transmissions. Big stuff. Hard-to-do stuff. Stuff that will require hiring, either for money or barter, a mechanic.

Stay away from dealers or major garages like they were the plague. It isn't just that they are a little too high—most of them are so expensive they amount to being ludicrous. Many dealers charge three to five *times* the going rate for a job and you get no more from it.

Look for one of those small, neighborhood

A SURVIVAL GUIDE

mechanics who work in a compact garage or operation. Get a written estimate on the job, and what it's worth—unless you have worked out some other kind of deal, of course—and then get down to work at it. Explain how you are living, with minimal money, poverty, etc., and see if you can barter something for the work. Cleaning up the garage, perhaps helping to work on your own car, anything that will lower the amount of money involved. Also, if you aren't sure, check to make sure the repair is absolutely necessary.

Often there might be a shortcut that will keep the car running. The classic example we found was when our new Pinto wagon finked on us and we went to a garage and were told that it would need a new carburetor kit. And true, such a kit would have fixed it. But so did spraying some cleaner down the throat; it fixed it fine, cost less than a dime, and lasted for another year. (Ultimately, of course, the kit would probably have to be installed. But to put it off for two or three years—that's effective shopping.)

Don't repair anything you don't need. If your car has air conditioning, for instance, and it goes on the blink, consider leaving it bad or taking it out altogether. Fixing it will cost time or money and probably isn't worth the doing. Same goes for minor body work, dings and scratches, or upholstery repair.

If it goes forward and backward, left and right, and gets you where you're going with a minimum hassle—that's good enough. At least if you're living poor.

A car can look perfectly awful, like something the cat dragged in, and still provide the same service. Spending a fortune to make it pretty doesn't help it's go-function at all.

Of course, the best thing to be able to do when it comes to automobiles is to get rid of the things. That sounds like a bit of a radical cure, but in truth it's much easier to survive without them than it is with them. The whole concept of the automobile has gone beyond sense, gone beyond any kind of reason. They cost outrageously to buy, cost more to run, and emesh the owner in a pile of licenses and insurance paperwork that is simply ridiculous. To truly live poor, it is almost necessary to either vastly curtail car use (once a week at the most—try for less), or to stop using it altogether.

After the first week or so, not using a car isn't so difficult and there are, in fact, side benefits that make it worthwhile. Walking or biking is healthy, at the start, but that's only part of it.

Three hundred thousand people a year are killed or maimed because of automobiles, or because of bad driving. If you don't drive your chances of being part of that statistic are greatly reduced, brought to nearly nothing. True, some maniac who is drunk can still run off a road and take you out on the sidewalk, but the odds are much better for you if you aren't in a car, aren't out where they can get a shot at you.

A SURVIVAL GUIDE

And it is truly awesome what you can do on foot once you get in shape and overcome the mental inertia of using a car.

Consider what we have lost. During the Civil War it was *common* for infantry to march seventy-five miles and then fight a pitched battle when they arrived.

Now, during training, they walk eighteen and feel as if they've accomplished something. And the same downgrade in physical abilities has reached all aspects of human living.

Walking a mile is, really, nothing. It takes fifteen or twenty minutes at a leisurely pace, produces no ill effects, and generally gets you to a store or market or work, if you live in a sensible town. But even in a city, two or three miles will cover most of what you need to do and that means you're only walking an hour at the outside to get where you want to go. An hour with no insurance to pay, no gas or oil to buy, vastly reduced odds of an accident, and the ability to do something that improves your health.

As to carrying loads while you're walking, there are several methods available. For smaller loads there's the backpack, or just a pack-frame. You can carry a surprising amount on a pack system and still be comfortable. For heavier loads you can rig up some kind of a two-wheel cart assembly, the kind that uses bicycle wheels and balances on two wheels. With one of those you can carry lumber, other building materials—

actually, almost everything you can carry in a car.

Then there are animals—horses, mules, dogs. They have all worked for man, and will work again. Of course animal use depends on where you live—a horse in the city is impossible these days. But if you are living on the outskirts or in a small town or out of town, give all thought to using some form of animal power rather than a car.

As previously mentioned we live far enough north to use sled-dogs. We have a cart that we use in the fall and spring (you can't run them in the summer heat), and then the sleds for after snow falls. We go everywhere we could have gone with a car, *including* downtown; do all our shopping with them, or what shopping we do, and have a lot more fun doing it.

It might seem strange to cover these alternative methods of travel in the section on automobiles, but it's done to point up the most important fact of automobile usage: to wit, if you're living as a poor person it's almost mandatory to give up the car.

Unless you are truly made of iron, you can't compromise—any use is deadly. In our case we tried to do minimal use of the car, tried to be sensible, but in no time we were using it more and more at greater and greater expense until we were starting to get caught in the same old money trap of having to have money simply to feed the car.

A SURVIVAL GUIDE

We were used to having it easy, that was our problem. We had it easy for years and years; when we broke away we found we could do without some of the façade of easiness—do without cars—except that if we tried to use even some part of it again, just a partial use of the car, we fell back into our old ways and rapidly disintegrated into living easily again. Much the way one knows an alcoholic can't take just one drink, that's the same way we had to leave the concept of the car.

If at all possible, even if you don't think you can, try to stay away from the chrome mastadons. The things never worked anyway, have always been a millstone around our necks, and they cost so much—not just in money but in health—that the very best automobile "repair" kit is to not have one in the first place.

8

HEALTH—THE BODY—CLOTHING—THE MIND—HUNTING DEALS

"The human body is greatly overrated."

Medical and dental problems occur even when you're poor. Teeth go bad, injuries come up, life goes on—although we have noticed that we are decidedly healthier poor, as already mentioned. The problem is that doctors and dentists seem to have such a massively inflated idea of their worth; same for hospitals.

As the saying goes, getting sick costs so much you might as well stay healthy. One visit to the doctor wipes out what a poor person can live on for a week. And if there is need of a hospital, it's like the national debt of a small country before you get out of the place.

The primary difficulty in dealing with medical problems is that most often real money is required. It's difficult to pay in barter or goods. You can try on the doctors and dentists. Barter food or services for their time, and often at that level it will work out. We've swapped cleaning services and food for dental care; ditto for country-clinic medical help.

In the case of having to have money, there are still some options open, or some methods available for at least alleviating some of the expense. First, as with all expenditures when you are poor, make certain you need a doctor before you go. When we became poor, and accepted it, we found that many of the apparent medical problems we had been suffering disappeared—problems we had gone to the doctor for previously. We had weight problems; I had blood pressure difficulties, stress—all of that is gone now, and without need of the doctor who we once felt we had to have.

We also go less in the case of injuries. Cuts that would have once sent us scurrying to the clinic we now fix ourselves. We keep a comprehensive first-aid system in our home and we disinfect, do our own bandaging, that sort of thing. Nothing major, but everything short of that, we do ourselves.

Just in these two areas we have cut back a decidedly large chunk of our previous medical expenses. In fact, just being careful not to go to the doctor until we find it absolutely necessary cut expenses back a good 60 percent—which is probably a true indication of our cultural paranoia more than anything else. But it is still a true figure. We used to spend horrendous amounts of money on unnecessary trips to the

A SURVIVAL GUIDE

doctor simply to compensate for the pressures of the way we were living. Now we don't.

When we do have to go, when there isn't a way around using money, we try to minimize the cost as with anything else. If it's the hospital, we just automaticaly say no to any of the options—television, private room, etc.—and try to cut corners whenever possible. This includes using "free" clinics and the like, if they're available, and as much out-patient care as we can.

Health insurance: We don't have it. Many people do, even poor people, but we have found that for the most part it's just too expensive for what you get. They want an arm and leg for it and then will drop you if you get sick; if you aren't constantly ill anyway they don't pay off. It's a losing proposition to give them the monthly payment unless you're figuring on something long and devastating, and then they won't take you on in the first place. Generally speaking, it's the same as with car insurance: Clichéd as it might be, if they can afford to take you on, you don't need it.

The Navajos have a concept that, very briefly put, says if you stand in good relation to your gods you will live better, in all ways. We have found that to be true medically speaking. We are trying to live within the framework of a sensible life, a reasonable life—a life based on reason—and our medical needs have correspondingly plummeted to almost nothing.

When we first started to be poor we saw a

doctor or the local clinic probably on an average of once every six weeks. Now it's once a year, if that.

Clothing.

Just in the concept of changing from status clothing (i.e., name brand) to buying sensibly, a tremendous saving can be realized.

We bought well-known brand names for years, and I firmly believed that they were better, aside from the fashion element involved. They weren't. Or, actually, name brands are often better, but if you sit down and work out the life of the garment versus the money it costs, you come out way ahead shopping for a good deal in new clothing.

Of course, we buy hardly anything new now. At first we had trouble doing that and thought we still had to have all new, and hence good, clothing. It was strange, but that for us was one of the hardest parts of the new poor life—clothing. Now we're fairly sensible about it, but when we first made the move, it was hard. Not that we were fashion plates or anything. But we just always bought new when we needed anything and to lose that concept was difficult.

Still, even having to buy new clothing there can be a lot of money saved by careful shopping. Stay away from brand names, look for discount sales, think in terms of minimal altering. A pair of jeans that are too long, but on sale, can easily be shortened, make the savings worth the work. Look for things that are too long and learn to change them to suit your needs.

Except for work boots, which must fit perfectly because we work and walk great distances, and of course underwear, we buy almost all our clothing used in secondhand stores and at rummage sales. By watching carefully we get nearly exactly what we want and the savings are fantastic.

Another good way to get really *good* clothing cheaply is army surplus. It might not be fashionable, but it's tough as hell and cheap.

Goodwill, Salvation Army stores, factory second outlets—there's always a place to get clothing at a reduced rate. It's just a matter of looking, or working at it until you find the way.

Dishes, cooking utensils, etc.

Most of this stuff you just have—or at least we do. We never seem to have to buy silverware or plates or cheese slicers or spatulas. It's always just there.

But if you need that sort of thing, including pots and pans, stick with rummage sales or secondhand stores. That stuff is outrageously priced if you buy it new and can be picked up for a song used.

Same for appliances. If you need them, for Heaven's sake stay out of the stores. Look for used ones in the newspapers or secondhand stores or wherever. Another way to go is to buy something that doesn't work and fix it up. This naturally requires that either you know something about appliances or are in a position to barter repair work for something you have.

But broken-down appliances can often be had simply for the taking away and if it's easily repaired—usually a motor or switch goes on them and can be obtained used—you wind up with a good appliance for nothing or next to nothing.

We haven't done it, but some people we talked to for the book said the best place to pick up used appliances is to look for homes that are being broken up. They swear that divorce sales are the cheapest because the people involved don't care.

The one thing we found not to do is getting anything hot. There is a regular commerce going on in stolen goods, it seems, and often chances to buy items that are stolen come along.

We found it best to avoid them for two reasons. First, the legality involved; if you buy stolen goods you're in a bad spot with the law, especially if you know or suspect they're stolen because they're so cheap. But more importantly, it's the concept of buying stolen goods that we found to be damaging. People we saw who stole or bought stolen goods were always looking for something for nothing, it seemed. Not in a good way, but in a way laced with greed.

When they got locked into that pattern it seemed to push them back into the kind of living and thinking that ruined them in the first place. We saw no exceptions to this and talked to (sadly) quite a few people who bought what might be called questionable goods.

Furniture.

A good amount of home furniture can be made, if you have a slight bit of coordination. But that which can't be made, or if you choose not to mess with home construction of it, can usually be picked up for nearly nothing at rummage sales or secondhand stores or the like.

We have found that mattresses tend to be lumpy when they are used unless they are reconditioned, in which event they cost a bit more.

We have also found that plastic-chrome-formica things tend to be built for one-family use. We're not paranoid, particularly, but my wife is convinced things of that nature are designed to fall apart in a certain time span and they do seem to work that way. Design or not, plastic-chrome things don't seem to make it when you buy them used. What happens, usually, is that the screws pull out of the wood particle board underneath all that chrome and plastic. You can semifix it by filling the screw hole with quick drying epoxy and then drilling a small pilot hole and rescrewing that part back on, but it will not be as good as the original and should only be done as a secondary way to get furniture.

In used furniture wood is the only way to go. Even if it's broken, with any of dozens of good types of glue it can easily be repaired so that the break is actually stronger than the original wood. A little sanding and refinishing and it will look as good as new—literally—and be at least as strong.

The main difficulty we've run into in dealing with used furniture is the kind that needs upholstering. At first we just assumed that it would be easy to reupholster the odd couch or chair and do all right. The first time we tried it we wound up with something that looked like a ruptured water buffalo. Considering that it started life as a small easy chair, this transition was even more notable and it was flatly impossible to sit on it. Or in it. Or around it.

Since that chair we have stayed with things we could either just clean up or, at the most, make a slipcover for; nothing we have to gut and recover completely. Maybe it's just that we aren't good at that sort of thing but I still have nightmares about trying to tuck padding into places where it refuses to go.

Televisions.

This, rightly, could have been under appliances, but in truth acquiring a television set is so singular that it should have a place of its own. First, consider not getting one at all. It isn't just that they are addictive, or seem to be. And it isn't just that the programming is so abysmal. It's the time.

When you are living poor and working at improving the quality of your life it takes time; not just time to work at things, but time to enjoy them as well. Perhaps a description of what I mean would be more appropriate.

When I taught at the University of Colorado I would spent hours teaching or preparing to teach for what amounted to so many dollars an hour. When I finished teaching for the day I would go home, stopping at the store on the way to buy preprepared food of one kind or another (usually fattening; often fried chicken or some other quick food), and after eating I would sit down and vicariously live by watching somebody do something on television. If I were in a daydreaming mood I would dream of taking a vacation to fish or hunt or go sailing or some such endeavor—quite often something I was watching the people on television doing.

Now I no longer teach at the University of Colorado, no longer earn so many dollars for hours of teaching, no longer stop at the store and pick up a chicken to eat while I watch somebody else do the living.

Instead I might, typically, hunt dinner, if it's fall. Or fish for dinner if it's summer. The same hunting or fishing I would have done on vacation except now I do it for food instead of stopping at the store. If I'm not hunting I might be taking dinner from our garden system, or working at my own food in some other way.

The point is that when you are living and not just watching somebody else live on the tube, it takes the time to live that you would have spent watching them do it for you. I might spend hours hunting, hours that I enjoy, to bring in a few grouse or rabbits or a deer; then more hours to process the meat and prepare it for either storage or cooking. Then still more time is spent cooking it and finally, best of all, the time spent eating it. Not during any of this, at no time in this whole process of living, have I got any time to watch some silly idiot jumping around shooting bad guys on the video screen.

We are too busy living now to spend much time watching television and I heartily recommend the same course of action for anybody else who is entering the world of the poor. If, however, you need a television or want one and haven't got one, the primary thought to keep is to stay away from color sets and stay away from new ones.

You can usually find a small used black-and-white for next to nothing at a rummage sale or auction. Plug it in, and make sure it works, and take it home if it does. If it doesn't work, leave it.

The whole area of fixing television sets has become such a dangerous one in terms of

A SURVIVAL GUIDE

money spent for value received that it's probably not worth doing. Even if you do the work yourself and if the problem with the set is just a few tubes, you can easily chew a massive chunk out of thirty or forty dollars. Since a new old one might only be ten or fifteen dollars, it's not economical to fix them. As for taking them to a repairman—not unless there are four men with ropes and tractors pulling you. And then fight like hell.

It is just possible that if you personally know a television repairman that it possibly would be viable to take a broken set to him for repair—not just know him, but perhaps are related to him. Say if he's your brother. Or your mother.

Under no other conditions should you take a set in to have it fixed at a repair shop. Horror stories abound about getting nailed by unscrupulous repair shops, and while it is not the purpose of this book to furnish and exposé of various industries, in this case it might be best to point out a fact: Out of all the people interviewed for this book who had work done by television shops, out of all of them, not one had anything good to say about television repair shops. And a lot of them had a lot to say that wasn't so good.

Using that as a guide be your own judge, and remember that from the standpoint of living a high-quality poor life perhaps having a television at all is not to be desired.

From the the standpoint of brands or kinds of

set there doesn't seem to be a whole whale of a difference. The same for American or foreign. We talked to people who had found used Japanese sets that lasted well and we talked to many who had bought older American sets that were still cooking along. Just be sure, when you get one, to test it before you hand the money over. There is a lot of scamming going around the world of moving used television sets. For a time a whole ring of con artists worked selling bad sets in good cartons, that sort of thing. Be careful and make sure it works, regardless of brand, country of origin.

And, finally, the same rule applies for "hot" sets as for stolen appliances. It's not particularly advisable to do it from the angle of the quality of your life, not to mention the legal side.

Stereos.
Strangely, at least for us, we have found it much more important to have high-quality listening than high-quality viewing and for that reason having a good stereo is important to us. My wife is an opera buff, I am firmly entrenched in Bach, and we have a large collection of records. So we worked hard and got a really good stereo system and spent quite a lot of money on it—just over a hundred dollars, used. We got it at a moving sale and I still haven't figured out why they didn't want to take it when they moved because it's a good set and rela-

A SURVIVAL GUIDE

tively small. We're glad to have it, however, and listen to it all the time.

If you are like us and need a good stereo, getting a used one is tricky. First, see if it works, naturally, and if it doesn't, see if there's a circuit breaker or fuse on the back that can be reset or replaced. Then try it again. Quite often a temporary overload will trip the breaker or blow the fuse. If it doesn't work still, it's a thorny problem because generally speaking the same people who fix television sets fix stereos.

If it is a very good stereo and you truly want it and it is a really good deal you might have to find a repairman.

There is one more option. See if there is a vocational school somewhere in your area that teaches radio and television repair. If so, talk to them and they might do it just for the cost of the parts. (You could also do this with a broken television, of course, but generally they aren't even worth the cost of the parts.)

If there isn't such a school, and you really *must* have the stereo, and your mother isn't a repairman, you might have to find one. Try asking people you know who have been to one and see if they can recommend anybody. Also check and see if there are any radio amateurs or the like around who work out of their garage and can fix your set in the evenings or, better yet, will show you how to fix your own set.

At the very last, when all other possible avenues have been exhausted, you might try the repair shop. And then, just before you go, call the Better Business Bureau and ask them to steer you clear of the worst ones.

Not to harp on these things but if a compromise does occur and you wind up spending a lot of money on something as small as repairing a stereo, it is very hard to turn it around. In our case we soon wanted to buy more and spend more on other things and though it stopped before it got out of hand, we came close to going back to the old way of living.

Living well, living with true quality, is a very fragile thing and easily destroyed. We have found that we have to work at it all the time, on all levels, to achieve success.

9

LIVING THE OLD WAYS

> "On a scale of one to ten progress comes in right at about two."

There is, as this is being written, quite a national movement to go back in time and live in the old ways. There are even clubs of people forming who hunt and live in primitive fashion—with muzzle-loading weapons, wearing buckskins—and not a few small farms that have rediscovered the horse as the primary form of motive force.

It works, it will continue to work, only on a small level. On an individual level. On an international level it is of course impossible to go back; international competition simply won't allow it. If we started using the bow and arrow again somebody with a gun would surely start to lean on us.

But on a selected basis, on an individual basis, it is not only possible but in many instances entirely desirable to go back in time to when there was a higher form of living quality.

The thing to do is to find that time, find that period of development in whatever it is you are doing when it was highest, and then adopt that period, that point in time.

As an example consider the concept of muzzle-loading arms. They were developed over hundreds of years, all the bugs worked out, and then dropped instantly when cartridge guns came along. The concept of using cartridges is still relatively new and still being worked out, and while it is true that they seem to be an improvement, that they are slightly more convenient, they have some deficiencies that are still being worked on.

Taken individually they are not wholly convenient. If you take a deer rifle out hunting, with high-powered cartridges, and decide to shoot a rabbit for dinner, there won't be anything left of the rabbit to eat when it's hit. To a certain extent muzzle-loading guns can be "tailor-loaded" in the field: a light load can be put in for small game, a large one for large game, and they become a more versatile weapon.

Or taken from an economic point of view, cartridge guns cost tons more to shoot than muzzle loaders. With a muzzle loader you can make your own bullets from scrap plumber's lead, buy black powder in bulk form, and shoot for only a small percentage of what it costs to

A SURVIVAL GUIDE

shoot conventional modern weapons. (Some people even make their own powder and save more.)

But the main idea is that a weapon designed over a hundred years ago—they are making exact reproductions now for comparatively little money—for all practical purposes is as accurate and as deadly as new weapons. Plus, it will probably be prettier, more versatile, more fun to shoot, and a lot cheaper, costing about a tenth as much to shoot. Older is better, in that one case, and for that narrow use of the weapon.

And that same rule applies to anything and everything. It is, for instance, not practical for the world to go back to farming with the horse—although with the energy crunch it's being reexamined. But for the individual small farmer, or a family living on a small farm, it is not only practical, it is advisable. You can grow your own "fuel" in the form of hay and oats; they are, for small uses, more versatile than a tractor; and as for maintenance and repair of equipment—it's simply not comparable. Tractors that break down, with the current cost of parts, might as well be left broken. As this is being written it costs more to just replace the starter on a tractor—actually, quite a small item and one that breaks down now and again—than it does to buy an entirely trained light-to-medium draft animal that can do most of the work on a small farm. Overhauling the engine on a small tractor costs more than it takes to feed a good team of fairly large workhorses for two or three *years*, and the overhaul expense doesn't take into account the continuing expense of fuel, oil, tires, and other equipment that wears out and can't be manufactured on your own, as you can repair your own harness.

On the other hand, there are some disadvantages to workhorses. They have to be fed all the time, even when you aren't using them, and they demand attention daily so you can't go off and leave them. And they must have shelter and training and. . . .

It is necessary, in this quest for the quality of the past, to evaluate each thing and decide whether or not it will improve your life and allow you to live well.

Our own case might be a good illustration. We threw off, initially, most of the shackles of the modern system. We have a hand-pump well in our kitchen (that we drove ourself, by hand), a wood cooking stove, and a wood heating stove, with no backup heat systems—fuel or electricity—to use. We have, in effect, disconnected from the oil companies—or to as large an extent as we can.

And we love it. We get all our own wood in, cut it, burn it on our own. The cooking stove furnishes not only cooking energy, but also some heat—actually a good measure of it. And if we get cold we have nobody to blame but ourselves. (We don't, typically, get cold.)

A SURVIVAL GUIDE

As for transportation, we did effectively the same thing. In the winter, when we have seven months of cold weather a year—we use a dog team. The dogs give us an honest ability to go fifty miles a day—more if we really need it—and we feed them with our own homemade dogfood (better than commercial). So we are not linked there to oil companies either. In the summer we use a horse and buggy, which is slightly more convenient than the dogs, but offers less in distance-covering ability.

We have, for all practical purposes, apparently dropped out of the system and gone back to a time when it was possibly to use your own motive force to get from one point to another, keep yourself warm, and totally feed yourself. And for those who are not afraid of work, I heartily recommend it as a way to live. In almost all instances, simply by living as they lived in the not too distant past, the late nineteenth century, we have improved the way we lived. We have in some cases dramatically, vastly improved our life—our food now is so much better that it really can't be compared. And our health—but we've already discussed that. By moving back, selectively, we have also to a large degree improved our family life.

We had moved apart, the three of us, and living as we now live has brought us back together. There is more unity now. We are all part of what we are doing, part of our life, and we have grown because of it. Not to get schlocky about this, but in a very real way that is what our life is all about. It was something we had lost living in a modern sense and something that has almost completely come back to us living the old way. Or living mostly the old ways.

It was, is, necessary to be selective about it, obviously. We had to pick the best place to live with everything we have used or lived with. We couldn't just go back to the fire and the cave and start knocking off saber-tooth tigers for dinner.

We decided on wood heat and cooking, for instance, because it gave us a measure of personal control over our own comfort. Yet for the cutting of that wood—we use ten cords a year—I opted for the relatively modern process of using a chain saw. Obviously, we have to buy gas and oil for the chain saw, and in that sense we still use the system; we haven't gone totally back to the past. And to be truthful we tried to go without it, cut all our wood with bucksaws by hand, but it took so much time that some of our other endeavors—hunting and trapping—suffered. So we used the power saw. We still only use a minimal amount of gas—last year, all year, four gallons plus oil—and that points up another facet of living in the past.

In those areas where it is necessary to come forward and live in the present, if you can minimize that impact it will help immensely, as with dealing with any other part of the modern—

A SURVIVAL GUIDE

hence expensive—technological system. In a very general sense, the reason it works to go back in time is that in the good old days—and they *were* good, cliché that it is—it was possible to use your work directly for the product you needed. If you wanted a home, for instance, you could cut logs and make one for yourself (illegal now in many states). You didn't have to hire a bunch of people and pay a bank rapacious interest rates and go into debt, literally, for the rest of your life. You just traded your work for a home.

That rule, the application of your personal work for the product you needed, worked all though the past because in many instances that was the *only* way to get the product. For that reason they knew more back then about how to take care of themselves, how to build and fashion for themselves, than we do now. They could, and did, everything for themselves and what they learned we can use now.

What is perhaps most indicative of the folly of progress is that *when* we use those old methods we most often come up with a better product at a cheaper price. Just this past summer I ran into an example of this that still makes me wonder. I was building a small, elevated food cache for storing dog food in the winter, a hut up on stilts, and I wanted to shingle the small roof on this hut with wooden shingles. I have never made shingles, knew nothing of it, and in a moment of weakness I took the team into town and went to the lumber yard to buy enough cedar shingles for the roof.

I was stunned to find that for the tiny roof the shingles, if I bought them, would come to over two hundred dollars. So I went home without the shingles. Instead I sent for a book on old tools and methods and researched how to make shingles.

It is easy to make them. Not only easy, but fun. You just cut logs in the correct length for your shingles and use a fro (a kind of long-bladed knife you can make easily) to split shingles off the log. I sat in the sun in a warm summer afternoon with a bunch of cedar logs cut up and in three hours split more than enough shingles for the roof on the food cache. And they were just as good as if I'd bought them.

In effect I paid myself close to seventy dollars an hour for going back in the past and using the old methods. And if you use that for a rough guide it makes using the past a little easier.

We have found that if we only use the methods of the past when it will improve the way we live or keep us from having to go back into the system for money, it seems to work out best. Of course there is the pleasure aspect of it as well, the aesthetic side of it; In our case we have come to use that as improving the way we live, so it still works out.

To harness the dogs in the winter when it is really cold and then to go the twelve miles or so to the nearest town, running silently through the white world—it is incredibly beautiful. To be sure, we still only go from home to town to pick up some trifle at the store, but the *way* we go now is so different, so cloaked in beauty that it has become impossible for us to come back to the present and lower the quality of our life.

Coming home one night after a film—in that same town twelve miles away—we were moving through a twenty-below world with a full moon splashing white on the snow and there was such beauty in it that I thought my heart would stop. I began to lean down over the back of the sled and say something to both my wife and son about it, then changed my mind and didn't because it would have been wrong to talk, somehow. When we got home my son went to bed, still silent, and we sat sipping tea and my wife smiled.

"Coming home, that was special."

I nodded. She'd felt it; my son had felt it, too.

It was a beauty, a joy that I have never, under any circumstance, felt driving a car.

And we have found that by living in the past that same beauty and joy has entered many other parts of our lives. It is definitely worth a try.

One bit of pertinent advice before you romp back into the past, however: Take it slow, one thing at a time.

We interviewed several families who tried going back in all ways all at once and it turned into a disaster. It's one thing to decide to cut all your own wood the first year, or perhaps go back to canning instead of buying at the store. Actually, doing either one of those can save you lots of money and be more work than you think.

But to decide in the same year to do away with cars and electricity, and to go back to canning with a wood stove and pressure cooker while hunting only with a bow and arrow and brushing your teeth with baking soda and using corn starch instead of talcum powder for the rash that comes because you're wearing home-tanned skins. . . .

It can be a bit much.

10

LEARNING OLD WAYS

"Everybody has to learn everything all over again. That's what makes the study of history so ridiculous."

One of the prime difficulties we faced—still face to some small degree—and see other people who are newly poor facing, is the concept of learning how to live of, by, and for ourselves.

So *much* has been done for us, over the years, by others—other people, outside systems, machinery; our abilities at many things have atrophied through uselessness the way a muscle will weaken if not used.

It's almost as if we had forgotten things culturally, or perhaps genetically. A built-in ignorance had overtaken us, and that—when being poor put us back into a position of actually having to fend for ourselves—was nearly crippling. It wasn't just that we had forgotten something we were supposed to have known—we never knew it.

BEAT THE SYSTEM

Wood Heating and Cooking

Take the burning of wood. We got a small stove at a rummage sale, hooked some chimney to it, and the first fall threw in some wood and lit it and expected to be warm all winter. It just never hit us that there would be a lot more to it than that. You got a stove, put wood in sit, torched it, and you were warm.

What we didn't know, what we have since learned, is that to get wood burning to work right, for heat or cooking is almost an art form. You can just throw in a piece of wood and light it and it will give off heat, at least to some degree; but if you know what kind of wood to throw in and how and when to throw it in and how to burn it after it's in the stove it can increase the heat tenfold— which is to say you only have to cut a tenth as much wood.

If you burn green hardwood, for instance, you get a slow heat until it dries out and triggers and then a short hot blast that only lasts an hour or so. Birch is the worst for this short-burning business—the worst of the harder woods, that is. On the other hand, burning green wood generates tons of creosote in your chimney that can (a) catch on fire and take the house with it or, (b) condense and drip down the stovepipe in a thick oil-tar solution that will literally, completely, dissolve a thin-wall metal chimney in a matter of a week or two. Creosote is nearly as corrosive as powerful acid and the first winter we wound up burning green birch and had to completely replace our chimney system four times.

Burning dry wood is far easier, which means if you cut it green you must cut and split it an entire season before you tend using it. That means you're cutting two years ahead when you cut, if you start green. But if you go with dead wood that is already dried in the woods but not yet punky or rotten, you will find the creosote problem handled—only dry wood burns so fast that it takes much more to last any amount of time. Also, the type of wood determines the amount, length, and kind of heat you get (dirty or clean, fast or slow). Poplar torches quite hot, burns very fast, and is good for getting an oven up to baking temperature or a quick blast out of the room heater to take the edge off a cold room. Dry, very dry pine does the same except that it smokes a bit more and if you haven't a good draft it can dirty the room a bit. Birch, dry, will last a bit longer than poplar, but not much, and smokes to beat hell because of the bark. Dry oak burns long and relatively hot and can be used for overnight heat fires or long baking (a turkey, etc.).

An art form, and one that we have basically forgotten. If you are cooking with wood, as an example, and are going to bake bread, the most efficient procedure is to start with pine kindling to heat up the steel and get the fire going. Then add dry-split poplar to get the oven up to the correct temperature (bread *does* bake better in a wood stove, by the way). Then put in dry oak, maple, or elm for the long heat of baking.

For heating a house you start with kindling to get the draft going, then lay a good fire with dry poplar or birch to get a proper bed of coals, and when that is burned down add your overnight wood—nonsplit oak or maple or elm—as big as you can get in the stove door.

Damper control on both wood cooking and heat is another part of the art form and can make the difference between kinds of heat and efficiency of wood use. By opening and closing the damper on a wood cooking range you can regulate the heat of the oven or cooking top within a few degrees, after a bit of practice, and make wood last eight or nine times as long. On a heating stove you can close it down and make a fire last for a full day or open it and get a blast that will make your stove glow red and warm half a block, it seems.

Also, height of chimney is critical. It must be a couple of feet higher than the peak of the roof for proper draw. If it isn't it might work for a considerable time and seem all right, but the first flukey wind that comes will fill your house with smoke and simply ruin your day. Or week.

A SURVIVAL GUIDE
Sewing

Another area where we had to learn everything all over again, culturally, was in sewing. We had always just bought new and didn't repair because it didn't seem economical. Then when we ran out of money, it was not only economical but necessary: A new pair of jeans costs more, right now, than we spend at the grocery in nearly two weeks.

So we tried hand sewing to fix things when they tore, and found, much to our surprise, that it's difficult to sit down and sew a good seam. You can throw a few stitches in and get something that might look all right, but to do a decent seam that will last on a pair of boy's pants for more then an hour is really tough. It takes patience, close stitching, attention to tightness—a lot of care.

And the first time we tried a sewing machine it would have made a good filmed comedy. We didn't get a new one, of course, just an old used one we picked up at a sale, and I thank Heaven for that: a new one, with all the dials and gadgets, would have probably seen us both committed to an asylum somewhere. It took, literally, weeks before we sould get the thing to work correctly, to sew a seam tightly; and the tinkering quotient was enough to make us stammer.

The trick, we found, with getting old machines to work right was in the tension—the little tension control knob that the thread goes through that keeps it coming at the right tightness. If it's too tight the thread breaks; if it's too loose there will be big loops on the bottom of what you're sewing. Use old cloth and check it many times before you start sewing for real, and then recheck it often.

Also, be sure you get a needle that's long enough. I didn't at first and found that if the needle isn't long enough it won't take the thread down far enough for the little arm to swing across and catch it with the thread from the bobbin.

The bobbin? Right. We didn't know about that, either. That's the secondary spool down in the guts of the machine that puts the thread on the bottom of what you're sewing and ties off the thread that comes down from the top. The bobbin has to be filled with thread, and there is another gadget over to the right of the machine that will flop forward and spin the bobbin spool so you can fill it off a regular spool of thread.

All of this sounds crazy, of course, and might seem minor, but an old sewing machine is usually the one you get when you are poor and when they are old they don't come with owner's manuals.

A most important thing to remember about old sewing machines, or anything from the near past, is to ask the man or woman who owned one. One of the best fundamental resources we have available to use in learning to live poorly

A SURVIVAL GUIDE

or learning to live in the old ways that were and are better—one of our *best* sources of information are the people who did it.

Senior citizens, older people, people going through their golden age—whatever or however you choose to term them, our older people constitute a staggering fund of information and knowledge that is, in some cases desperately, waiting to be tapped.

Time and again we have run into corners of our own ignorance, only to be saved by older people when we asked them for help. Use of old machines, cooking, canning, slaughtering and cutting meat, hunting, fishing, training horses and dogs, using harness, using old woodcutting tools, burning wood, growing our own food—the list is endless. And in each category when we had trouble we went to older people, sometimes at a nearby nursing home, and swapped food or time or help for information.

It is truly amazing what they know, what they can tell you, what they can save you in time and effort and pain, just for the asking.

On sewing machines, for instance, we finally ran into brick walls that just wouldn't fall. I had worked and tinkered on the needle for weeks and it wouldn't work. The machine wouldn't sew.

Five miles south of us lived an old farm couple, and through the grapevine we'd heard that they were getting rid of a pile of aged manure we needed for our garden. While there—we took some pastry and had coffee with them, or tea—I happened to mention the sewing machine. It turned out she had owned the same exact model when it was new. In no time she'd filled me in on the fact that my needle was too short, and many other things I was doing wrong. She also told us much other that we needed to know to live our new-poor way and her husband, who took a bit longer to warm to us, finally opened up and I am *still* working at some of the information he told us about working a small farm with horses, fishing, weather forecasting—tons of knowledge. And what we've checked seems to work out well.

He told us that when it is a new moon, if the moon is rocked on its back so that it would hold water it will probably be a dry month. If it's tipped forward so it will drain out it will be a wet one. And the same holds true for the big dipper in early evening. And it works. We've checked it now for a year and a half and it's surprising how often it's correct.

None of which has anything to do with sewing and yet has everything to do with sewing because sewing, as with so many other lost abilities, is so directly linked with older people: They wait to be asked and can help so much *when* asked that it's astounding.

A SURVIVAL GUIDE
Keeping Warm

Perhaps this might have been covered better in the wood heating section except that it's an old art unto itself: staying warm without expending money-requiring energy.

First, primarily, most important: USE SOMEBODY ELSE'S HEAT, if at all possible.

Near where we live—well, twenty some miles—there is a middle-sized American town of about nine thousand souls. They have an old-fashioned library with high French-paned windows. One day I was in getting books and noticed a dozen or so older women, seated, knitting and crocheting in the sun at the tables beneath these windows. I remarked how charming it looked, the light streaming down on them, and asked if it was a club or group or something.

"No," the librarian told me. "They come here to get warm. They can't afford to turn their thermostats up to a comfort level at home because of the energy crunch. During the day they turn their thermostats down and come here to sit and be warm."

It was of course midwinter—fifteen below outside—and it is not the intent of this book to get into any heavy messages about what filth the large energy conglomerates have become (they are doing that nicely for themselves, actually). But the plight of the older ladies and their solution to that difficulty is a good example of

BEAT THE SYSTEM

the best method of staying warm with somebody else's money.

Libraries are good for that, depots, museums—anywhere you can go and perhaps sit for a time and read, or enjoy what's there and be warm without actually spending your own money to get warm, will work.

So does clothing. Wear it in layers, with long undergarments and shirts and sweaters, and take them off or add them as you get too warm or too cold. By working for a time with layering and doing a little experimenting you can find just what it takes to meet various requirements, and after that it's easy.

Feet, hands, and the head are the vital areas to keep warm, even in the house. There is a marvelous sketch done by Whistler showing one of his friends sitting in a cold apartment in London. The friend is also an artist and is doing a sketch of his own, but what is notable is the way Whistler's friend is dressed. He's in sweaters and a wool cap with a large muffler, and he's wearing those woolen gloves with no fingers while he is sketching. There is also a large comforter wrapped around his legs, and you can almost feel how cold it was in the apartment.

It is, of course, an overstatement. But it shows perhaps the best method of staying warm without spending money. Dress warmer than you think you'll need, most especially inside. In winter dressing for outside you naturally dress warmer, but it helps to dress warm for the inside as well. Take a hint from Whistler's friend and for each step you turn the thermostat down add another layer of warm clothing. It costs nothing to wear clothing for comfort; it costs a fortune to turn the heat up, a fortune in fuel bills.

In winter, unless we're using our hands, we wear cheap cloth gloves and sheepskin slippers inside, putting them on as soon as we get up. I also wear a woolen watch cap and have found it to make a tremendous difference in maintaining my body heat. We heat with wood, but by staying warm inside our bodies we can greatly decrease the amount of wood we burn. I figured it out last winter, and by wearing light gloves and warm slippers and woolen caps we saved nearly two full cords of wood. Twenty percent. If you can work a 20 percent discount in your heating bill simply by wearing a few more clothes, to hell with fashion.

And finally, eat well. Typically, primitive northern tribes ate fatty foods to stay warm and if it doesn't play the devil with your diet you might do the same. If you exercise a great deal and burn it off you won't get fat and you will stay warm. But in the absence of eating a fatty diet, eat well and often and do as much physically as you can.

Given proper diet and clothing, the human body is a grand heater and will take care of itself admirably. All it needs is a little help. Start with clothing and work out.

BEAT THE SYSTEM

When you have good clothing and you still want to keep the thermostat down further, began to close off areas of the house or apartment. Close heating ducts to rooms that aren't needed for the winter, then close and tape and seal the rooms. Be sure to tape across the bottoms of the doors. If it's electrical heat turn off the zone for the cold room and seal it off.

Don't heat anything you don't need and don't waste the heat you have. Make sure you have storm windows and then cover with plastic and seal that tightly as well.

If there is a draft, a small movement of air, find where it starts and stop it. Keep at this all winter, taping holes—we found them around light switches in some apartments, around outlets as well—wherever you might see them.

We had been, in our upper-middle-lower class days, heat gluttons. We kept our house warm night and day, all barrels going full blast. We kept the thermostat cranked up and we could walk from the tub barefoot into the bedroom after a bath in midwinter and not feel the slightest discomfort. That cost us just over two hundred and fifty dollars a month and had to change when we got poor.

Now we spend a little extra time dressing as soon as we got out of the tub, bathe with water heated on the wood stove, and save all that money.

Just by keeping warm in the old ways.

A SURVIVAL GUIDE
Clothing

Methods of getting inexpensive clothing have already been discussed elsewhere, but knowledge about how to get clothing to last and work right for you is from the past and one of those things we seem to have forgotten.

Basically, the thing to remember is that wherever clothing wears it can be repaired—especially with children's clothing.

It was once customary to put double layers of cloth at wear points—knees, elbows, and bottoms. For whatever reason they have quit doing it, but it is important to keep in mind that it works. Double layers at the knees will add tremendously to the length of time the pants last and if you add the second material on the outside as opposed to on the inside you will never really get down to wearing at the original material.

If you're not particularly concerned at how it might look, it also helps to make the secondary material some extra-tough stuff. Some used soft or smooth leather or heavy canvas or corduroy. You can sew patches on knees with a machine after tearing out the inseam. Then sew the patch in and resew the seam. (I worked for a long time to get to that bit of information—kept trying to ball the pants leg up and around the arm of the machine, thereby proving that you don't have to be smart to be poor. Just smarter than it takes to be rich.)

BEAT THE SYSTEM

Don't throw anything away. Old jeans are especially good for this double-layering work. The same for old boots or shoes; the leather will be good for making clothing tough.

And making clothing tough is what's needed to avoid spending vast amounts of money on worn-out knees.

Shoes

In shoes or boots the word is TOUGH.

Much has been done for fashion in modern footwear and most of it is only good for that: looking at it. But it doesn't last.

The exception to this is some of the craftsmanship done in work or hiking boots with the cleated soles. They are already tough and will last a long time but, most important, THEY CAN BE REPAIRED.

There's the rub. Many shoes and boots made today are virtually not repairable. Whether intentional or not, this built in self-destruct system on footwear means that it costs too much because you have to keep buying shoes.

When you get shoes or boots make sure the sole plate is *sewed* to the upper part, and not just glued. If it's glued you can't resole, if it's stitched you can. With good upper leather, well rubbed with preservative oil (there are many good ones, but if nothing else shortening works pretty well and keeps it soft and noncracking), a

A SURVIVAL GUIDE

pair of work boots might last a decade. They used to in the old days.

Also, don't neglect to patch and sew the upper parts if they wear or get cut. If you don't want to spend the relatively small amount of money needed for shoe repair—or can't work out a bartering system with a shoe repair shop—you can stitch the leather with heavy needles and a thimble and thickish, strong waxed cord. It's a little difficult, but it can be done—using scrap leather from old worn-out boots and shoes—and with minimal practice it's surprising how tight and usable the repaired leather can become.

Making shoes and boots tough—assuming they are leather, and none of the present synthetics work as well as leather for wear and comfort— is really only a matter of good care. Make sure the leather isn't allowed to dry out by rubbing in oil (do it often), and patch it or repair it just before you think it's really necessary. If you repair soles before they are worn away, the upper part won't deteriorate. If you wait until that heel is all ground down it will start to wear away the leather of the upper, and reshape it the wrong way and ruin the boot. Fix it just before it becomes an emergency.

You can, if you wish, double the leather at the wear points and then only keep replacing the worn secondary leather. The insides of the heel go fast on most boots, and the toes, so extra leather there would help.

Before we entered the throw-away generation

most farms and homes had cobblers lasts, little iron upside down feet that could be fastened down on a bench or stool and used for home shoe repair. Until fairly recently home shoe repair included redoing soles, heels—the whole works. You can still find those lasts at sales and auctions—indeed, they are one of the most common items in antique stores and secondhand shops. If you want to try it you'll find it fairly easy to glue on new soles (with good leather glue) and nail on hew heels (you can also glue them). Try on an old pair before you tear into your good boots. There are some tricks to it and practice makes it a bit easier.

While on shoes it might be salient to point out that for casual wear you can make your own moccasins or sandals. There are many patterns (look in appropriate how-to books in the library) and they work surprisingly well. We even do our own mukluks, using old Eskimo patterns, for winter use and they compete well with commercial shoe-paks or felt lined boots.

Moccasins wear out fairly fast, especially in urban use where there is much walking on gravel or concrete. But if you have a good pattern to start with and leftover leather, you can make new ones for much less than you'd expect to pay for materials. A whole tanned hide of good cowskin will make many pairs of moccasins and the hide costs much less than a single pair of good hiking boots. The work of making shoes or moccasins is painstaking, but with a little time and effort it's possible to do a creditable job.

Tools

Elsewhere we have discussed building homes and doing your own repairs or remodeling. It is assumed before you do some of those things that you learn about power tools and the like, work with them, be completely familiar with them before using them.

But this section deals with learning the old ways with tools, the old methods of tool use, because old tools and the rebirth of doing things the old way demands that old concepts and knowledge be reborn.

Hand tools, be it carpentry or mechanical, came pretty close to not being used anymore. Power has entered everywhere, and everything. The idea of hand sawing or planing wood has given way to power saws and power sanders, and if you have a lot of work to do in a small time, maybe power is best.

But care of hand tools, care and proper use, is something that must be relearned if you're going to do things the old way. For that reason, the following might help.

Care of old tools might best be summed up in that one word: *care.* Modern tools, like so much of our modern society, tend to lean towards the no-repair, throw-away-when-worn concept. Many power saws, for instance, *can't* be repaired and must be discarded when broken; they have sealed cases.

Old tools were made to be repaired. Perhaps that should be amended to state that not just older tools, but new tools made in the old ways are made to be fixed. The key to repairing anything is to use a program of *care*—preventive maintenance—to avoid breakage in the first place.

When you acquire an old-new tool take it completely apart, clean it well, sharpen it if it needs it (as with a plane or a saw—or have them sharpened); then lightly oil the metal parts to prevent rust before putting it away for storage. What's more, follow this procedure every time you use the tool. It takes a lot of time, but in the end it's well worth the work and the tool, if it was in good shape in the first place, will last your lifetime.

That's a good thing to think about. When you get new-old tools and you take the time to make them right, it's very good to think that as you work it will make the tool last the rest of your life.

It is also good to think about that when you are using the new-old tools. There is an art to using, say, a plane that demands patience and a kind of love. When you work at it and practice you can feel when it goes from work to becoming an extension of your hand—a definite step.

A SURVIVAL GUIDE

It's a feeling that will last the rest of your life.

All tools are different, of course, and will demand different forms of use. For specifics about using old tools you can check the library—there are many different kinds of planes, as an example, and whole books on just how to use them. Or you can find an older person who knows how to use the specific tool you are using and barter food for knowledge.

But there is a general thought that applies to all new-old tools and their use, something we have forgotten.

First, they used to build things to last, not to be done in a hurry. Somewhere along the way we dropped some of the quality and went for the speed and we have suffered because of it—much of what we do now doesn't last. A table topped in plastic with fiberboard base just won't last. A hand-rubbed plank table will be around for your grandchildren to use and the extra time it takes to make it with hand tools, old tools in the old ways, is well worth it. Second, it isn't the end of the journey that counts, it's the trip.

We have become achievement oriented. Somehow, we have come to believe that the end of the journey, the end of our life, the end product of whatever we are doing, is the most important thing.

We look for the pot of gold at the end of the rainbow and miss the rainbow. And it is the same with the old tools, working with them the old way.

In our rush to speed we have lost the joy of work; we have lost much of the fulfillment that can come from using hand tools. It can be sensual, alive, and very gratifying in the sense that you are almost sculpting. Using hand tools in the old way is an art-craft that is well worth the relearning. It's like relearning to look at the rainbow.

Pets

Perhaps in no other facet of the human spectrum has so much money gone into so little true product as when it comes to dealing with pets—cats, dogs, and whatever other animals that have changed from livestock into closer domestic ties.

Special beds, leashes, "cute" toys, diets, supplemental vitamins that aren't, so-called special foods—the pet business is so big that it's hard to measure it.

What we seem to have forgotten about pets is that they are essentially the same as they've always been—they are animals.

They need good food, shelter, and decent care and affection. Any further attention goes beyond sense and most certainly goes beyond being poor.

Of all the considerations of pets, perhaps the most insane is pet food. As this is being written pet food in cans costs more than many kinds of good human food. Maybe this is just as well because it pushes some of the sad people who eat pet food back into eating human food, which is better for them, but it's also sensible because it drives people away from spending needless money on pet foods.

You can, most decidedly, make your own.

Take dogs. What they do with dry dog food is grind up various grains (corn, wheat), mix it up with various kinds of meat and fat (you wouldn't want to know where it comes from), press it into little pellets, and dry it. Sometimes they add some vitamins—not necessarily everything needed—and that's it: the pet diet.

Cat food is essentially the same thing. Odds and ends of fish and chicken guts are added, stuff nobody else can or will eat, and it's named something Madison Avenue-cute and costs so much it's ridiculous.

Point: If you eat a well balanced, rounded diet and have a small dog, the dog can get by nicely on table scraps. If you have a large dog and want to increase the amount you feed the dog, make up your own dog food.

A recipe (we use it for our sled dogs) is below:

> Dry materials: Mix half-ground wheat, ground fine but not as fine as flour, and half-wheat middlings; also 4 percent brewer's yeast. (All these things can be purchased at the local feed mill.)
>
> Add enough warm water (about 120° F.) to turn the grain mixture into a thick porridge.

BEAT THE SYSTEM

Mix in table scraps, meat (without bones), vegetables—whatever you've got. Put it aside to brew for 24 hours and use the day after you mix it. Feed it to your dog moist, as the digestive system of the dogs seems to get more food value out of moist food.

Cat food is a bit more complicated. While I tend to be pragmatic about cats and not put up with any of their temperamental nature, my wife insists that certain cats need certain food. Since she's the cat person it's probably best to use her methodology.

You can, however, still make your own. Buy cheap fish (or catch your own), and mix it with table scraps. You can also buy chicken or turkey parts to mix with cooked potatoes and come up with a passable food. We met one family that feeds their cats raw gophers and other pests they trap, and some merely feed their cats table scraps and allow them to hunt their own food (although, to be honest, we saw some pretty thin and wild-looking cats—I wouldn't have tried to pet them without a whip and a chair).

Bird food is essentially grains, and you can get the ingredients off the package and do your own easily.

Rabbits will eat almost anything and if you can find some grass or clover or corn stalks or surplus cabbage you can keep them well fed.

No matter the pet, check the ingredients on

the commercial feed and make your own. Under no condition use the commercial variety because you're just paying somebody else to do your work for you.

11

RIB-STICKING RECIPES

"In the end, it is only necessary to eat."

At the start of the book we discussed stretching out with a meat and potatoes emergency get-along meal. And to be sure, many cultures get along on a much worse diet than meat and potatoes; in rough times people have lived on virtually nothing, and have gotten by.

Still, variety is nice, and so is functional nutrition. Just getting by does ruinous things to a balanced diet and health can drop pretty fast. It's a very good idea to bring in outside dishes to add to your staples—things like fruit and vegetables and dairy products that have lots of vitamins.

But, in the concept of being poor, there is a whole new approach to eating that needs study as well as a few recipes. First, cooking limited little gourmet meals with specialized courses is naturally out. It costs too much. Whether it's store-bought food or food you've grown or raised yourself, using it up in fits and dabs for temporary pleasure just isn't economical.

Generally speaking, it's better to cook large amounts and eat it for several days or freeze it or save it another way for eating more in later meals. Let's say you come into some steak—either you get some beef through barter or kill a deer. Steak is very good meat, and in the way of such things it is usually obtained in very limited quantities. To take this very good meat and consume it in an orgy of barbecue self-gratification, or charcoal it all for one meal, is plainly a waste. Wonderful, delicious—but a waste.

A steak can be "stretched" by many methods to pull the quality into many meals so that you aren't using it up all at once. The taste can be pulled from it and made to reappear again and again in making other meals not just nutritious, but good tasting as well. The same for other meats, or cheeses.

Meals can last for days. It is just a fairly recent turn in human history that makes us think in terms of cooking for a single meal—part of the fast-food syndrome. In the very recent past it was common to keep a pot of something cooking—a basic core for meals, which could be added to if necessary as the situation demanded. Often a thickish soup, perhaps an open-ended stew that could be increased as it was depleted—these basic pots could be used for days, even a week, just by adding to them as they were depleted.

These are the meals of the poor, the true meals that last and provide substantial food for a long time; the good meals.

Following are some recipes for long, good meals—lengthy food.

Beans

Soak a huge pot of pinto beans and cook them until they are done. If you use your own home-grown pintos you'll find the taste to be so much better than store-bought it's frightening— what do they *do* to the beans in the store?

Add chunks of cooked meat or cooked hamburger. Adding not just the meat, but the grease the meat was cooked in as well. Then add two huge onions, chopped. These are also much better if they come from your own garden, but it not, buy two big ones. Or barter for them.

Allow this bean pot to cook slowly all day. Not really hot cooking, just simmering. (It works best on a wood stove.)

The resulting pile of beans is a good stock, a good basic food that will last days and days and can be used as a central core for many different meals. As might be suspected, however, it will be almost insufferable bland—just a kind of filler.

But if you add some tomatoes, it will magically turn into a chili base and if you throw in some red peppers you will have a really good chili. Or if you cook it until it thickens it can become a surprisingly good substitute sloppy-joe material. And if you cook it still further until it forms a paste, it makes good substitute meat. In a sandwich with home-grown lettuce and tomato, it's almost like barbecued beef.

Or, you can go ahead and have one meal from the bland pot, then freeze the rest in bags for future use. Or you can add some garlic and sprinkle a little cheese on top, and it comes out with an Italian flavor. Somehow.

Thin it with water later and it's a very good bean soup. Add that same garlic and pepper to the soup and it becomes zippy and new. These things can go on, adding and changing the basic bean pot to meet new requirements.

You can also add as it goes, add beans and new meat to keep the pot going, as they used to in the old days. We have kept our bean pot going, active on the stove, for two weeks and it just got better all the time. While doing research we talked to one couple who just kept their pot going. Period. They had no idea how long it had been on the stove because, as the woman said, "It's always there."

That's the key to a good bean pot.

It's always there.

It works for all kinds of beans. Not just pintos but navies. The same basic pot will keep going, although other kinds of beans make for strange chili. Edible, but strange. If you take a bowl of those little white navy beans and serve it with one piece of crisp fried bacon on top and some grated goat cheese on top of that, it's nearly divine. Served hot on a very cold day when you come in off the dog run with your belly dead-empty, such a thick bean soup makes your soul sing. For those who are vegetarians, replace the bacon with a long, thinly sliced piece of potato fried super-crisp in vegetable oil. This procedure with potatoes also works for simulated bacon-lettuce-and-tomato sandwiches.

Soups

Probably the most traditional long-playing meal is soup. It is most certainly the classic meal of the poor, along with beans, because traditionally it has been economical to make.

The reason, of course, is that short of using wood you can make soup out of nearly anything.

Put it in a pot, add water, heat it up, and you've got soup. Generally speaking, the better the quality of the materials you put in, the better the quality of the soup you get.

Still, there are some basic soups that lend themselves to taste, to getting better as time goes on, and to sticking to your ribs.

We usually start with a nonstrong vegetable base. Carrots, some diced potatoes, celery (all home grown) and often, though it's a bit strong, some shredded cabbage. Unless it's to become a stew or stewish base, we stay away from turnips or rutabagas.

To this possibly bland base we add seasoning. We all like black pepper so we cook that in, and enough garlic so our dogs duck when we lean down to harness them.

But that's just the base. If we wanted specialized soups we will remove some of this large initial pot and make smaller soups for individual meals. Clam soup (as opposed to chowder) is a big one for us, using well washed freshwater clams from nearby lakes. Another is onion—we just add some diced onions to a smaller pot and cook as onion soup.

Somehow, we've found that the basic stock, which we might keep going on the side of the wood cooking range for weeks, will adopt the taste and feel of the specialized soups.

We can also add meat—often ruffed grouse, perhaps rabbit that has been prebrowned in homemade butter—and if it's left thin it's a good meat soup from that same basic stock.

Allowed to cook down and thicken, as it does naturally over a period of days, and with meat added, it can make a delicious stew. And, finally, we do a thing called trapline beverage.

We take the stew, cooked way down, and run it through the blender with a little added warm water to make a liquid that we then heat piping hot and put in a thermos for use on the trapline. It's a sure-fire way to cut 20 below weather when we stop to give the dogs a break and we don't have to start a fire to have a hot meal. It's also a good meal in a duck blind or in the pack for cross-country skiing—a kind of stew you can eat without a fork. (This blender business also works with other forms of instant meals for trail use.)

Meat Base

To stretch a good meat into many meals we cut it into small pieces or grind it up and fry it in a pan with a semineutral oil, like corn or sunflower. When the meat is fried we add water—just half a cup or a little more—then separate this prefried meat and the juice equally and store it in small freezer bags.

Each of the little bags of meat and juice and frozen oil is the core for a whole meal of meat and secondary food.

We've found that if we use just the juice mixed with refried beans, and then fry the beans in little patties, they become something very close to tasting like the original meat. This leaves the meat to be fried in oil again and mixed with a bit of water one more time, then made into soup or stew or thick gravy to be put over boiled potatoes or thick buttered slices of freshly baked bread.

We're not sure of the record, but one family, who gave us the original recipe for this meat base, made a small steak last four months. And they got the piece of steak at a sale for out-of-date meat in the first place.

We didn't try it with chicken or pork. Chicken is a little risky because it's kind of a marginal storage meat after it's cooked. Pork would probably work if you trim off all the fat, which could give it an off-taste after a long time. Of course, smoked ham lasts a fairly long time and there is fat on it, so it might be worth a try. If not precooked, pork can be cut up in small pieces when it's raw and frozen in small amounts and stretched that way.

DON'T TRY THIS WITH FISH: You can freeze fish raw in small freezer bags with a bit of water around the pieces and it will taste fresh months later. But spoiled fish can cause death really fast, so don't get too exotic without checking carefully first.

Stretching works really well with lamb, however, probably because it has such a distinctive taste in the first place. Fried patties of premashed potatoes come out tasting like lamb chops, sort of—if you use your imagination a lot.

Game Stew

You can, as with soup, make a good game stew with nearly any kind of game. In doing research we found people who used bobcat, while one practical soul used a domestic cat and swore that it tasted fine. Others actually used skunk; some made a stew with fox meat (for anybody who has ever skinned a fox, this takes on real meaning—they smell worse than skunks); many used rabbits; not a few used porcupine, squirrels, pheasant, turkey (wild), venison, woodchuck, prairie dog, ground squirrel, and (I couldn't do this) gopher.

Clean the animal, whatever it is. Put it in a pot and preboil it just a smidge (a couple of minutes) to take out a lot of the so-called gamey taste. Then fry it until well browned.

Put chunks of this game into a pot and add enough water to cover. Then throw in some small-cut bits of potatoes and maybe some turnips cut into small pieces. Also some carrots, if you like, or anything else that sounds good. Cabbage tends to be a bit strong though, and will dominate and ultimately conquer the stew.

When you get enough of what you want, put the pot on a back burner, add water to cover the contents if necessary, bring to a boil, then cut back and simmer until you're bored.

Then simmer some more, and still more, into the second and third day, adding water and eating out meals as you go.

Days, weeks, down the road it will taste better than it did when you cooked it in the first place. And if you want to add game as you go, it's a simple matter.

Whatever you shoot or trap or get, clean it well, cut into small chunks, brown it well—actually cook it until done—then add it to the game stew. It will cook in as you go and you can come up with some pretty distinctive-tasting dishes as the game mixes. Grouse and rabbit becomes grouse. Throw in squirrel and it turns into something that tastes not unlike duck, for some reason—that's if it's a small red squirrel. If you use larger grays or foxes; it's still grouse-tasting except that it has a smoother texture.

Venison can, of course, make a stew something probably immoral. If you take the tough neck of a buck deer and cook it for two or three years, it will make a passable burned roast. But if you take that same neck and cut most of the tallow off (it makes good candles, by the way) and put it in the stew pot and add a ruffed grouse. . . .

There is no way to adequately describe the taste that comes from such a stew, especially if eaten in the cold of late fall after a day of cutting wood or after walking home from an old-fashioned library with high ceilings and quiet reading rooms—walking home in the cold with good books, which you can sit and read while sipping the broth from the game stew.

Things can all tie together when you are poor, tie together in good ways that do not involve money. Somehow game stew goes with cutting wood and old libraries and good books and cold cheeks.

It is also very good after making love under large quilts in a room, with a potbelly stove that has a window, where you can sit and sip the hot stew with lots of pepper and melted homemade butter and study the flickering yellow light and try and remember why it is you once wanted to be rich.

But that's a matter of personal taste and most certainly something you will have to find out for yourself. Game stew is very good for helping you develop personal taste.

Bread

There are, literally, hundreds and hundreds of bread recipes. Many of them, most of them, are delicious and some of them are actually nutritious as well as being good-tasting—although nutritious bread is not as common as good-tasting bread.

We use a very flexible concept because as poor people we sometimes don't have everything that goes into it.

Start with the correct amount of dry yeast— one of those little envelopes or, if you're buying it in bulk, a level tablespoon. Mix it up with a quarter cup of warm water (not hot, it will kill the yeast). Set it aside.

In a big bowl mix three cups of warm water (if you have milk, you can substitute one of the cups of water with warm milk) with a couple of tablespoons of honey and less than a tablespoon of salt. You can, if needed, leave the salt out. If you wish to add anything personal to make it a unique recipe now is the time to do it: special seasoning, maybe garlic; sometimes we try a little pepper or molasses. Things like that.

When you have the liquid mixed well you put in the yeast mixture and stir, then add half the flour and stir it in. On the flour start with four cups, mix it in, than a couple more cups and see how it's going. You usually use seven to eight cups of flour. Altogether: Seven in the bowl, and one on the board for kneading.

About kneading: You just keep flopping the dough over and pushing it into itself with the backs of your fists until it's like a baby's bottom, except that it doesn't come back out when you pull your finger back—sort of.

The eighth cup of flour is sprinkled on the board as you knead to keep the dough from sticking to the table. When you finish kneading you put it in a greased bowl (use margarine and rub it on with your fingers) until it rises to double in size. Don't panic if it's not exact. This is just a rough approximation.

When it's roughly double punch it back down and then separate into three equal loaves—they will be tiny little things—and put them into three pregreased single-loaf bread pans. These will make smallish loaves, but it seems to work out best for meals. One of the loaves takes us through a day—breakfast, lunch, and dinner. You could, of course, double the recipe and make six small loaves and freeze them, but we like to have the smell of baking bread more often and also get the taste of fresh bread. You can make triple the recipe as well, just by tripling everything, and freeze it before baking and save them to bake later. It will taste pretty fresh, but we just like to do it more often.

The whole thing, making and baking bread, is kind of a statement of life for us—a feeling more than just eating. It is a thing we do once every four days to fit into all the other things we do, a part of our journey, a part of our rainbow. But it can be varied if you wish to fit convenience needs.

When the small loaves are in the greased pans, stick them in the oven to rise. Turn the oven on to the very lowest position, leave it on for a minute, then turn it off. This will warm the oven enough to get the yeast to rise properly. If you get it too hot it will kill all the little buggers and you'll get bread you can use to fix truck tires.

When the bread has risen to even or slightly above the edge of the pan it's time to bake it. Preheat the oven to 350° F. When it's hot, pop the pans into the oven (marvelous phrase, that, and one that appears in all the homey cookbooks; "pop the pan into the oven"—I love it) and bake until done. This takes about twenty to thirty minutes, depending on your oven. But temperature indicators are so notoriously different that you almost can't go by them at all. The bread, when done, will have a golden brown crust over the top, will have risen majestically in a crown over the top of the pan, and will have a smell that will drive your saliva glands into high gear. Also, take one of the pans out with a hot pad and turn it over gently. The loaf, if done, will virtually fall out into your other hand.

We always eat one loaf fairly hot, cut with a hot knife (it kind of tears and looks bad but we don't mind), and smeared with homemade butter and honey.

It's hard to write about it without feeling hunger pangs. I mean, it's just an incredible experience, hot fresh bread with homemade butter and honey. It's also delicious with homemade peanut butter (just put some shelled peanuts in a blender and hit it, pushing down with a spoon). And if you have a slab of venison roast and put it on a piece about an inch-thick dripping with that same homemade butter, add some salt and pepper and just bite and chew. . . .

Well, some things are too personal to write about. But it's one of the few things that can rival love. Maybe it *is* a kind of love.

And that's bread.

Back during the recipe we kind of glossed over a vital fact. To wit: flour.

You can make bread with any kind of flour. Not just wheat but rye, oats, bean flour, or mixes of any of them—one company made bread with wood, as we've already covered. Bread is just something you do with ground-up grain and indeed, if you want to have a good time, you might experiment with different kinds of flour. I especially like about half whole wheat, ground fine, and half rye, ground just as fine, with a little molasses.

But the main point with flour is that the food value of the bread you wind up with is totally dependent on the flour you put into it. If you get bleached commercial flour, then you wind up with bleached bread that has about the same food value as bleached rice—almost nothing.

Whole wheat flour, while it makes darker bread, is a lot better for you from the standpoint of nutrition than bleached white flour, obviously. But sometimes it's a little hard to sell it to children (our son doesn't like the brown color or the slightly coarser texture).

We have found a new kind of flour that is essentially whole wheat except that it's ground really fine and makes a kind of golden bread that has the same texture as the pure that word sure is out of place with white bread, isn't it?) white flour makes.

The most important thing is to get the best-tasting, most nutritious bread you can get for the money you spend on flour or grain. (We have started to buy whole wheat from a nearby farmer and are grinding it up with our own hand mill, which saves a vast amount of money, but takes some work.) It's silly to spend money or barter on something that's absolutely without any food value, so work at it until you find something that gives you a good basic bread for your needs.

Then work at it until you get a good bread. Don't be discouraged if it doesn't turn out right at first. All ovens are different, as are bread pans and dough consistencies—even altitude will have a bearing on how the bread turns out. Stay with it.

Universal Sausage

Soup, stew, bread, sausage—these are the fundamental, basic core foods we use to keep us going. And of all of them the one with the most rib-sticking ability is the sausage.

We're not talking now about the ground-up breakfast sausage that you buy, or get when you have somebody else grind up your pig. That's a specialized form that, aside from being good-tasting, is a monumental waste of meat and fat. It's too limited a use for it.

What we're talking about here is the same concept they use commercially when they make sausage, bologna, or hot dogs—that sort of thing, except that we're not going to use the same ingredients they use.

The whole initial idea behind sausage, aside from being an old-fashioned way to preserve and store meat, is to use up those things that you might normally not have a use for. And not just meat, either. It's possible, even easy, to make sausage out of almost anything and that's also the basic key to making sausage. With the exception of squishy vegetables—squash, or saucy things—save all leftovers for sausage.

Especially save all meat and fat scraps, anything you think won't go anywhere else. And if it should not work well in sausage, use it in your pet food or use the blender to turn it into something for trail use.

What we do is make a base potato sausage, using ground up spuds as the main ingredient. We've found that if we do it right the potatoes take on the consistency of meat and take on the taste of whatever the other ingredients are.

First, it's necessary to have a meat grinder. We scrounged one for a quarter at a yard sale—it had a little rust, but steel wool cleaned it off nicely. But even if (shudder) you have to buy one new, it's mandatory to have one. Actually, they're so handy to have around that you might as well pick one up anyway.

Next, go to the store and get sausage casing. These are pig guts, to be blunt, that usually come in a little box. There is enough in one of the little boxes to probably last you for two or more years. The casings are well washed, packed in salt, and don't look or feel bad, so even if you're squeamish it shouldn't upset you. Set the box in the refrigerator for the time being.

Third, you need a tapering funnel for stuffing the sausage, unless, of course, you've got a stuffer with your meat grinder. Assuming you haven't, you can usually make a good stuffer out of an old piece of horn (if you're in the country), or a piece of plastic if you live in a city and can't come across some horn. This stuffer should be slightly tapered, be about one inch across at at the narrowest end and about an inch and a half at the big end. It's not a wild funnel, almost a straight tube—indeed, if you can't find anything funnel-shaped, or make anything, a straight piece of plastic tubing one-and-a-quarter inches across makes a usable stuffer. Use a piece of sandpaper to clean and round all inner and outer edges.

Making the sausage: Peel and quarter five pounds of potatoes. More if it's a big family or you want to store sausage for a long time; but start with at least five.

Using a relatively coarse blade (or one with big holes in it if you have that kind of grinder), grind the potatoes. They shouldn't be processed into mush, but should be kind of gritty—not big chunks, either. Right in between.

Put them either in a bowl, a colander, or other screened object in the sink, and let as much of the starchy fluid drain off them as possible. As a matter of fact, when you are done grinding pick up the potatoes in small handfuls and mash them together with a patting motion to squeeze out any further water. This makes them less fattening, which is a nice side benefit, but by squeezing the fluid out of them they become more receptive to picking up the flavor of the seasoning and meat in the sausage.

Next, grind up the leftover meat, or raw meat scraps, or cheap stew-meat, or (for five pounds of potatoes) about two pounds of fatty hamburger. (Is there another kind these days?) Also grind up three large onions—they'll mush up a bit, but it won't matter. It's the flavor you're after.

A blender won't work for all this. We tried it. I won't go into details except to say that it doesn't work.

Seasoning: It's pretty much a case of what do you have that you want to put in a sausage. The traditional potato sausage is really bland and it's served with seasoning on the table, but we like to heat it up a bit with various spices. And we change it all the time.

Usually, however, we'll load it up with some chopped red pepper, maybe a little green; more than three onions; some finely chopped celery; half a ton of garlic (well, quite a bit—as much as you can stand). Also, maybe, some ground-up black pepper, two or three cups of fresh frozen corn. Plus leftover cooked meat, etc.

All this should be hand-mixed well with the ground-up raw potatoes. Stir it in with your fingers, squishing it back and forth, squeezing it through itself over and over until it's well mixed. Then do it some more. Maybe throw in another mixing about here— set it aside and prepare the casings.

Take a piece out of the container and wash it

well in cold water. It's already clean of the gooey stuff from when it was part of the pig's guts; this washing is to take the salt off. When the outside is clean, pour cold water through the inside as well. It's a bit difficult to find the opening at the end, but keep picking at it with your nails and it will open up. Then pour water through a couple of times to carry the salt out.

When it is well cleaned you might return and mix the stuffing material up one more time—it's really hard to mix it up too much.

Next, take your stuffing funnel, open the end of the sausage casing, and feed it up and around the funnel, all of it. The idea is that all the pig gut will be around the tube of the funnel and you'll feed off that as it's stuffed.

Holding the stuffer in your left hand with the casing around it, with a little tail of the casing hanging off the end of the tube, use your other hand to take a handful of your premixed sausage material and jam it in the open end of the funnel. Using your thumb, push it down the tube so that it starts to fill the gut. Then take another handful of material, feed it into the funnel, and pack it through with your thumb.

As it comes out the other end it will pull the casing off the stuffer, feeding as it goes. The idea isn't to pack the casing tight—when it cooks the material inside will expand to fill the sausage casing—but just to make a snug tube. It varies slightly, depending on the size of the gut, but if you keep it about an inch and a quarter in diameter you'll find it comes out right in the end.

Now you just repeat the process until you've used up all your gut and stuffing material, and you have feet and feet of sausage.

We've found it effective to take fishing string or some other strong string and tie it off every foot—we pinch it down and tie it in two places, so the two ends of each piece are tied. That sounds confusing but when you tie you'll see what it means. One-foot sections seem to work out for storage and quantity per meal.

When it's all stuffed it will seem a bit loose, but don't let that bother you. Set it aside for the moment.

Get a large pot and half fill it with cold water. Add sausage until it comes just below the surface, so all the sausage is still covered, and set it on to boil, going from the cold to boiling while the sausage is in the water. If you get the water boiling first and then add the sausage, it will burst.

Length of time for primary cooking depends drastically on your personal taste, the altitude at which you're cooking, and I think, the speed at which it goes from cold to boiling.

For the first batch try twenty minutes. If you cook it too long it will burst—not explode, just quietly rupture—and if it's cooked too short a time it will taste like raw potatoes. You might try a short section the first time to get the time down.

BEAT THE SYSTEM

When it's cooked right the potatoes sort of disappear into a kind of meaty substance. They are still there, and there is still a touch of potato taste, overcome by the onions if you used them. But the texture of potatoes is gone and it's more like a soft sausage.

You can eat the sausage at this stage. Just serve it with small bowls of melted butter or margarine and put lots of seasoning on top of the butter, like pepper and salt.

But we usually freeze it. It keeps for months when wrapped and frozen properly (see any cookbook for storage of frozen food). And if you take a two-foot section of this sausage and fry it up for breakfast, fry it just past golden and into brown, and serve it with a couple of eggs and a bit of whole wheat toast, it will keep you going all day.

You can also take them frozen, put several sections on a pan, cover them with dry mushrooms and some sauce, and put tinfoil over them; bake them for twenty minutes and it's a whole meal. Or boil them wrapped around a venison roast . . . ah, yes, just writing about it makes the mouth water.

The point is, you've taken looked-down-upon food—potatoes and scraps—and turned it into something very close to a gourmet meal. That is the essence of eating when you are poor—use less money and still improve the quality by trading off work for quality.

And there are other benefits. The food is

A SURVIVAL GUIDE

healthier and you get the knowledge of having made your own food—a kind of fundamental joy.

While we were working on this, we were visited by a woman friend who is a writer of fiction and lives in a city environment.

She is a wonderful person, one we love very much, and we wanted to make her happy, share our best with her. So we decided to show her a truly good meal that doesn't come from anywhere but the heart, the soul.

We got four grouse and stuffed them with celery and corn and a touch of onion, surrounded them with freshly picked new potatoes, smothered them with homemade butter, steamed them under aluminum foil for twenty minutes, and then baked them open until they were golden going on brown.

We served them with hard-chilled fresh milk in frosted glasses and a sauce made from tomatoes and peppers and a little honey.

The idea is to take a piece of the grouse breast, wipe it in the butter at the bottom of the plate, and then dip it in the sauce and chew it hard before you swallow it. Then you take a sip of the cold milk and start over, alternating grouse and potato as you go, dipping the potato in the same butter and sauce.

It is a special meal for us, one we do when we start feeling like we need that yacht or two cars or all of that other junk that can lure you back into the trap.

BEAT THE SYSTEM

I put the grouse pan on the table and we started to eat, formally at first, then with open joy as the tastes and smells took us. When we had been eating for ten or fifteen minutes, I looked up and across the table and our friend was crying, openly weeping as she chewed.

"What's the matter?" My wife put her fork down. "Is something wrong?"

Tears came down. She shook her head. "No. Nothing. It's just so good and so beautiful and . . . oh, hell, *I* don't know. It's just that you have something I don't understand and don't think I'll ever have. I love you."

It's not just food. It's a way to live, a way to be. We are more now then we've ever been. She saw that and felt what we were, through that one meal.

That is the concept of eating when you are poor.

12

HOW TO LIVE ON JUST ABSOLUTELY ALMOST NOTHING

"There are murderees and murderers. At some point in life it is necessary to make one's choice."

We are living in a time of amazing changes. Of course, the same could be said of nearly any era, and yet there seems to be something about the last part of the twentieth century that makes it different from all previous ages in a unique way.

Technology, speed, information storage, production ability—there are many facets of our present time that combine to make it special. But the most distinct part of it, I think, is the fact that we live in a time of almost massive paradox.

It is a time of unbridled wealth and abundance—thanks to technology, so rich that it has never been equalled in history. At the same moment in history, it is a time of such stunning poverty and starvation that it cannot be believed. While some in our country eat bread made of wood, others—old people in the cities—are forced to eat canned pet food to survive. We have starvation occuring at the same time—in some cases, in the same states—in which we have so much food surplus it sometimes rots in the fields.

We have poverty at the same moment when there is so much wealth it cannot be imagined, cannot be counted. While some, many, most cannot afford to pay their heating and lighting bill, the people responsible for those bills, the energy conglomerates, are so rich they almost literally cannot measure their wealth; they pay people high wages just to find places to spend the money.

Paradox. And one that, historically, probably cannot last. In other times when such paradoxes were allowed to even begin, long before they got to the present level, there was upheaval. Usually violent upheaval.

And yet. . . .

Because of the advance of technology, because so much can be done so much easier, never has it been so easy to live truly well without any money. That, to me, is probably the greatest paradox, and also probably the reason there has not been a major upheaval.

Given necessity, purpose, and drive you can live now on nothing—literally nothing—and live much better than, say, a king in the Middle Ages. You eat better, are healthier, have better

A SURVIVAL GUIDE

hygiene, have better entertainment, have more knowledge, live longer, and enjoy easier living in modern times in crushing poverty than many—most—of the royalty of the Middle Ages. And that, as they say, is certainly something to think about—something to remember when it seems like you're between the rock and that proverbial hard place.

It is also something to think about if you must become a survivor—somebody who just lives, gets by, never has anything and must live on literally nothing.

Elsewhere in this book we've discussed getting down to nubs, really chewing close to the bone, but the presumption was taken that there would be something, some ability, some drive, some small or large thing that could be done to help out. A cottage industry, selling your body to science—always something.

It is possible to survive, to live, with nothing. Absolutely nothing. It is not to be recommended. If there are children or other family involved, it most certainly is not to be recommended. Sometimes there are not three squares, sometimes it gets a little hard for kids.

But. . . .

As an exercise, as a way to get knowledge of yourself, to see how you can do, you might try it. Or (harder to believe), if you just simply can't get any welfare or help or food or anything from outside sources, and have to do it because you have no choice. Do it.

BEAT THE SYSTEM

Just don't spend any money on anything starting immediately and see what happens. (Actually, while doing research, we went for an extended period spending nothing—also to re-restablish our value system more realistically—and were surprised to see how easy it is; almost too easy.)

Below are some mini-hints, things we used to survive. (Remember, pride is no part of it—if you have pride it becomes very difficult to make it. But then if you have pride it becomes very difficult to live in any way as a poor person. Aside from being ridiculous, pride has a way of just ruining the hell out of good poverty.)

Eating

Bluntly, relatives, friends, and neighbors—if you have no place to live you probably haven't got a garden, and assuming you can't work at a farm for food or some other way, cut way down and start making the rounds. We knew one person, an artist, who went for over a year without buying a single morsel of food and without growing or hunting his own. He ate with us often, more often with his parents, frequently with friends, and just kept moving on this cycle. Now and then he would miss a meal—and he rarely ate breakfast—and often he would have to eat something he perhaps didn't like all that much. But he ate for a year, ate whole meals, without ever spending money on food and with little effort. It can be done. Of course there are problems—it takes a lot of juggling, for instance, to keep those meals coming in and to keep all the relatives from talking to each other about you and cutting you off.

The thing about eating is that you've got to get to a point in your life where you make all your own food. It's all well and good to joke about eating with relatives and friends—or in all seriousness, to go ahead and ride the chuck circuit for a while. But to ultimately live without spending any money, you've got to wind up growing and raising your own. Period. Unless you're into stealing, in which event you'll ultimately get caught and get fed free. That isn't bad if you like boiled cabbage with a rubber spoon.

Shelter

To get food free, or just for labor, it's mandatory to get a place to live with some dirt. Soil is everything. Without it we are nothing, are dead and dust and gone. We must have it as a culture and that need can be brought down to the individual—down to you.

To live free you've got to grow food and to grow food you need a place to live where you have some soil available, or a place to live where it isn't too far from soil you can use or lease-rent for part of the crop.

In the summer, or in the more temperate regions of the country, you can, of course, camp. Or you can try to find a place to take care of—house-sit—or something abandoned that you can fix up for rent payment. There are many ways to get free housing—review the earlier part on housing for specifics. But the most important thing is that when you get housing there will be some dirt available for growing food.

Shelter can be almost anything, and that should be your guide in finding a home for nothing. Even if it's a stretched tarp, you can get by until you find something better.

But it must be within walking or wheelbarrow distance of dirt that can be used for growing food. Then restudy the early part on gardening, being sure to have at *least* three thousand square feet of usable soil—more if you can get it.

In an urban situation you can live where there isn't any soil and commute on foot, by bike, or by hitchhiking to get to the garden plot. A point to remember is that it isn't necessary for the dirt to all be in one spot. If you can't get enough soil in one place, have two or three plots—just check around. It isn't necessary that it all be in one lump, only that there be enough total soil area to grow enough food for a year.

Note that discussion of shelter eventually becomes a discussion of food.

A SURVIVAL GUIDE

We haven't changed in thousands of years. Almost everything about us is the same as it was in prehistoric times—all the modern trappings are just a façade. We must be with the food, move with the food the way ancient small tribes moved with the animal herds or migrated with the seasons.

In the end we scrabble, either as individuals or as whole cultures; in the end it comes down to a scrabble for food, a movement with the food sources. We just haven't found a way to live without eating.

And, in fact, that brings up the only real thing necessary for living with absolutely nothing—or at least the only new thing that makes it any different from living in normal poverty.

You must adapt the mental attitude of a survivor, if you haven't done so already. You must be ready to scrabble, to keep thinking and taking advantage of opportunities, to keep working at it—not just physically, but mentally.

Everything else—the mechanical means—has already been covered earlier in the book; at least the basics, the way to start.

But this mental attitude—the shift to learning to live with nothing, learning to survive—is not something that can be taught. It has to be learned by experience, by doing, and all the research, all the people we talked to pointed in the direction of specialized effort. It's different for every person and every situation and the only thing that really counts is making it.

BEAT THE SYSTEM

As one woman told us: "Everything changes as your belly starts moving towards your backbone. Everything."

And perhaps that is a good thing to think about in all aspects of learning to live lightly.

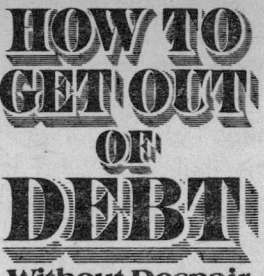

HOW TO GET OUT OF DEBT
Without Despair and Without a Lawyer
by Daniel Kaufman

Here is a straightforward, easy-to-understand guide for anyone who wants to stop worrying about debts and start doing something about them. Find out:

- How to inventory your assets
- How to make yourself judgment-proof
- How to identify and deal with your most important creditors
- When to see a credit counselor
- How to make your own debt payment arrangements
- When—and how—to declare bankruptcy

Learn about your legal rights and obligations as a debtor, and discover the options that will enable you to get the bill collector off your back—for good!

☐ 41-197-9 HOW TO GET OUT OF DEBT $2.50
Without Despair and Without a Lawyer

Buy them at your local bookstore or use this handy coupon
Clip and mail this page with your order

PINNACLE BOOKS, INC.—Reader Service Dept
1430 Broadway, New York, NY 10018

Please send me the book(s) I have checked above. I am enclosing $_____ (please add 75¢ to cover postage and handling). Send check or money order only—no cash or C.O.D.'s.

Mr./Mrs./Miss _____

Address _____

City _____ State/Zip _____

Please allow six weeks for delivery. Prices subject to change without notice.

HELP YOURSELF
To Bestsellers from Pinnacle

☐ **40-624-X How to Sell Your Film Project**
by Henry Beckman (hardcover size) **$9.95**
An indispensable handbook for writers, directors, producers, and investors. Everything you need to know in planning and producing a motion picture—from checklists to contracts to budgets to production.

☐ **74-014-X How to Get Out of Debt** (hardcover size) **$7.95**
☐ **41-197-9 How to Get Out of Debt** (paperback size) **$2.50**
by Daniel Kaufman
A simple, step-by-step guide to identifying your liabilities, tallying the pluses and minuses, dealing with creditors and setting up a sound program of financial recovery.

☐ **40-918-4 Shiatzu: Japanese Pressure Point Massage**
by Anika Bergson and Vladimir Tuchak **$1.95**
The ancient technique that will give you freedom from pain and tension—without drugs or special equipment.

☐ **41-032-8 12 Weeks to Better Vision**
by Barbara Hughes **$2.50**

Throw away your eyeglasses forever! Barbara Hughes shows you how to apply the world-renowned Bates Method to restore your eyesight with these easy-to-follow eye exercises.

☐ **40-629-0 The Complete Guide to Children's Allergies**
by Emile Somekh, M.D. (hardcover size) **$7.95**
An essential reference for parents of allergic children, written by a practicing pediatrician. Includes allergy-free diets, clothing, emotional problems, analysis of drugs, a glossary of terms, causes, care, cure—and more.

Buy them at your local bookstore or use this handy coupon
Clip and mail this page with your order
PINNACLE BOOKS, INC.—Reader Service Dept.
1430 Broadway, New York, NY 10018

Please send me the book(s) I have checked above. I am enclosing $_____ (please add 75¢ to cover postage and handling). Send check or money order only—no cash or C.O.D.'s.

Mr./Mrs./Miss _____

Address _____

City _____ State/Zip _____

Please allow six weeks for delivery. Prices subject to change without notice.